For Barbara
my wonderful ♡
here's to living our
lives of joy
& sharing
them
fully supported
by our special circle.

♡ Kay

Positively Brilliant
Self-mastery

Reclaim Your Authentic Self Now

[signature]

PETER J. REDING

Positively Brilliant Productions
La Mesa, California, USA

Category(ies) – 1. Self Help; 2. Personal Development;
3. Psychology (Self-knowing);

Positively Brilliant Self-mastery
Reclaim Your Authentic Self Now

Printed in the U.S.A.

ISBN-13: 978-0-9819108-0-2   ISBN-10: 0-9819108-0-7

Published by: Positively Brilliant Productions
http://www.positivelybrilliantproductions.com

Book Design by www.KarrieRoss.com

Library of Congress Control Number: 2008942413

January 2009

10 9 8 7 6 5 4 3 2 1

Disclaimer: This book is intended for those who have taken, or are ready to take, full responsibility for creating their own life. The Principles shared in this book are based on the author's personal experience. Your choice to use (or not use, or abuse) these Principles, is an individual and self-responsible decision. It is not the intention of the author to dictate to anyone how they should lead their life, what actions they should take or what path best serves their personal journey.

To Marcia Collins,
the most fascinating person I know
and
the person who models
Positively Brilliant Self-mastery
for me every day.

Acknowledgments

I acknowledge my family members as they continue to support my life's work. Thank you for your love of learning and your modeling for me to see the best in each person.

I acknowledge each of my extraordinary coaching clients who have entrusted me with holding their best and brightest selves. Their lives have positively touched tens of thousands, and one of those lives is mine. Thank you for reminding me what living your own life with passion looks like.

I acknowledge **Coach For Life**'s comprehensive Life Coach Program™ Graduates and accredited CLC - Certified Life Coach Program™ Certified Graduates. I acknowledge my colleagues in the **International Coach Federation** and the **Association of Coach Training Organizations**. My combined professional coaching community has been a source of support and inspiration. Thank you for the constant reminder of the human spirit's infinite potential.

Finally, I acknowledge the exemplary contributors of the stories for this book. Thank you for sharing your vulnerabilities and your triumphant Self-mastery. I list each contributor at the end of this book.

CONTENTS

SECTION I

YOUR INFINITE DIVINE NATURE 23

We explore our Divine Nature and how it *supports and informs who we are.*

You are connected to an infinite and life-affirming Divine Source (God, Higher Power, Spirit).

Your Divine Nature is resourceful, whole, and complete.

You have direct access to your Divine Source anytime you choose.

SECTION II

YOUR CREATIVE HUMAN NATURE 43

We explore our human nature that embodies our

human beliefs and attitudes. As humans, we have a choice of living by life-limiting beliefs and attitudes or *life-affirming beliefs and attitudes.* When we choose *life-affirming beliefs and attitudes,* our Divine Nature is expressed through our human nature.

YOUR LIFE-AFFIRMING BELIEFS

You believe that when you are connected to and guided by your sense of the Divine you are infinitely resourceful.

You believe that when you bring your Innate Gifts to your Innate Life Purpose as you honor your Innate Values you are living your Positively Brilliant Self.

You believe that when you acknowledge yourself for living your own life you are reenergized to contribute even more of you to your world.

YOUR LIFE-AFFIRMING ATTITUDES

You love and accept who you are right now.

You take responsibility for creating your life.

You focus on the positive in yourself and others.

SECTION III

We explore the Divine endowment of Innate Values that provide our most authentic way of *being*.

Your Innate Values are an endowment from your Divine Source.

You know your Innate Values.

You live in alignment with your Innate Values.

You acknowledge and celebrate living in alignment with your Innate Values.

SECTION IV

We explore the Divine endowment of Innate Life Purpose that provides our most fulfilling *direction and way of service*.

Your Innate Life Purpose is an endowment from your Divine Source.

You know your Innate Life Purpose.

You live in alignment with your Innate Life Purpose.

FOREWORD

*T*his book is written for you and those people in your life when you or they are looking for greater clarity or deeper meaning about who you really are.

This is the first release in the *Positively Brilliant Self-mastery Series™*. This book describes a foundational framework to guide you back to your most authentic Self. While simple and easy to understand, this book is powerful, practical, and empowering.

There are five planned releases for *Positively Brilliant Self-mastery – Workshop in a Box™* in this *Self-mastery Series™*. Each *Positively Brilliant Self-mastery – Workshop in a Box* will include a detailed workbook, audio tracts, a self-assessment, and a Mastery Journal that are collectively designed to support your discovery, integration, and celebration of one of the five major areas of your Positively Brilliant Self.

For most of your lifetime, you have been told who you are, what you need to do, and how you are supposed to be.

When you have not followed others' guidelines or mandates, you have been told you are doing your life wrong. Or more accurately 'you are not correctly following what others planned for you and your life.'

Going through a divorce, the loss of a loved one, a major change of lifestyle, being fired, downsized, or retired, or facing a significant health-related challenge can trigger a desire to embark on a deeply personal exploration. At these times of external crisis or internal breakdown, you may very well find yourself asking, *"Who am I? What is my purpose? Why am I alive?"*

You may even be asking, *"Am I worthy? Am I deserving of love? Do I make a difference in this world?"* [The answers to these last three questions by the way are Positively Yes!, Yes!, and Yes!]

Even when life is not as turbulent, there is an internal quest within each of us to *"know ourselves"* and *"live in alignment with ourselves."*

I share 21 principles that will guide you to access, re-evaluate, and align with who you really are. Your Positively Brilliant Self is within you right now. Your Positively Brilliant Self-mastery journey awaits . . .

Self-mastery is
Knowing, Living, and Celebrating
Your Innate and
Positively Brilliant Self
—Peter J. Reding

 n 1985, I was living in Tokyo, Japan. Well, in 1985, I was mostly a workaholic without an actual life. At 37 years old, I was incompetent at living my own life. Everyone else had defined, or dictated to me, who I was, what I needed to do, and who I should be to be successful, earn a good living, be promoted, and generally get ahead in this world.

I was very successful in getting ahead in this world. My world was international business. I was earning more than $100,000 a year. I was on the corporate management fast track. I could and did travel anywhere in the world I wanted to go . . . And I had no idea who I really was or what I was really meant to be doing. Twenty-three years later, I know who I really am. Now I am competent to live and celebrate my own life.

But in 1985 I was lost. The one place I had never visited was that deep place inside me that I believed was a dark and frightening abyss.

From my journal on November 30, 1985 - Tokyo, Japan

Say what others want,
even when it hurts my self,
I don't rate a 'Self'

Do what's expected,
to keep everyone happy,
(but do not count Self)

I'm so frustrated,
I could scream, better not scream
I might hurt someone.

Trapped to please them all
I broke the façade, and their
rules. Now free and scared.

I felt desperately isolated and empty inside. I was barricaded behind a 'façade of worldly success.' My compulsion to please others had preempted me from really knowing myself. If it was possible to convert self-worth to net worth, at 37 years old I could not have afforded the price of a 320-yen subway ticket to travel five kilometers from the Tokyo Station to where I worked.

The past 23 years have been a quest to know:

- How do I connect with my Divine Source?
- Who am I?
- What's my purpose?
- What are my natural gifts?
- How do I want to live my life?
- How, where, and who am I guided to serve?

What I've Learned

1. There has always been a part of me that really knows who I am, and you have this, too.
2. I can reconnect to my Positively Brilliant Self whenever I am open and ready to do the work, and so can you.
3. Knowing, living, and celebrating who I really am have changed every aspect of my life for the better. The journey into your self can be as meaningful and as fulfilling for you.

Positively Brilliant Self

I created the term *Positively Brilliant Self* to capture the concept and, for me, the reality that as a human being I have a human nature and at the same time I am endowed by my Divine Source with a Divine Nature.

My Divine Nature provides life-affirming clarity, direction, and resources to my creative and positive human nature. My Divine Nature is able to provide these things by being the reservoir of three major endowments from my Divine Source. The three endowments are my unique:

1. Innate Values,
2. Innate Life Purpose, and
3. Innate Gifts.

The Challenge

Your Positively Brilliant Self has been buried under what others have told you who you are. You are not, at least not entirely, what others have told you who you are. In some cases, you are not at all what others have told you by their words or actions toward you.

What others have modeled and told you have established your mostly unconscious, personal foundation. Your personal foundation tells you who you are, what you value, what purpose you pursue, and even the talents you should develop.

You have taken the sum of all these influences and have been going about your life, your relationships, and your career with a personal foundation that has been adopted from others. Part of your foundation may have served you and may very well continue to serve you. However, until you reconnect and remember your most authentic and Positively Brilliant Self, you are not, in fact cannot be, living your own life.

Until you reconnect and remember your most authentic and Positively Brilliant Self, you are not, in fact cannot be, living your own life or obtain any form of Self-mastery.

By not living your own life, you will continue to experience struggle, and/or burnout, and/or doubt, and/or unworthiness, and/or resentment. The grand booby prize includes feeling unfulfilled and knowing deep down inside you are missing something that is vital to your very existence.

There is a yearning voice within you calling to you to know who you really are, to live in alignment with who you really are, and to use your Innate Gifts to serve your Innate Life Purpose in your world and . . . at this time.

The Journey Begins by Knowing Yourself

Know thyself.
—Socrates

Get to know your most essential Self, authentic Self, true Self, or as I have come to call it, your Positively Brilliant Self. I guarantee there is a beautiful, valuable, and magnificent Self within you that is ready to be found and fully lived.

The principles I have used myself and have taught thousands of others who in turn have supported tens of thousands since 1996 are shared with you in this book.

The step-by-step, proven processes to know your Self are further shared in the *Positively Brilliant Self-mastery Series* offerings.

The Journey Continues by Living Your Own Life

To thine own self be true.
—William Shakespeare

Once you know who you really are, you can choose to align your daily life decisions and actions with whom you know yourself to be.

This book shares the principles of how to align your life with each of the easy-to-understand Principles that, when practiced, bring you to your *Positively Brilliant Self-mastery*.

The Journey Includes Celebrating Your Own Life

Celebrate yourself every time you catch yourself living in alignment with your Positively Brilliant Self.
—Peter J. Reding

Celebrating an act of alignment strengthens both the original conscious choice to align and what was being aligned. This is how positive new habits are formed and living your own life is forged.

What you acknowledge expands. Acknowledgement is another form of celebrating. When I acknowledge myself for knowing and living in alignment with my most authentic Self I am energized to live even more of my most authentic Self.

The Five Keys to Positively Brilliant Self-mastery

1. Connecting to your Divine Source
2. Choosing life-affirming beliefs and attitudes
    a. Your life-affirming beliefs
    b. Your life-affirming attitudes
3. Knowing, living, and celebrating your Innate Values

4. Knowing, living, and celebrating your Innate Life Purpose

5. Knowing, living, and celebrating your Innate Gifts

This book and the *Positively Brilliant Series* of books, products, and services are designed to inform, encourage, empower, guide, and support your lifelong journey in knowing, living, and celebrating your innate magnificence. You are Positively Brilliant. You always have been. You always will be.

Now it is up to you to know your most authentic Self, live your own life, and celebrate your Positively Brilliant Self. You are the only one who can make this deeply intimate and fulfilling Self-mastery journey. Allow me to be your guide.

Many people are now experiencing a greater sense of Self-mastery by continuing to follow the Principles discussed in this book. Some of their stories in their own words have been included in this book. Their stories help to illustrate a particular Principle. I hope this book and their stories inspire you along your journey of Positively Brilliant Self-mastery.

Peter J. Reding
San Diego, CA
July 1, 2008

TERMS

"Divine Source" – God, Creator, Higher Power, An infinite and life-affirming guide that is always accessible.

"Divine Nature" – That which comes from your Divine Source. The part of you that is Divine, Infinite, Holy, Perfect, Whole, Complete and Unchanging. Some refer to this as your Soul or Essential Self.

You are endowed by your Divine Source with Innate Values, an Innate Life Purpose, and Innate Gifts. You are equipped for life with the following:

- What you are here to *do* or *contribute* during your lifetime (your Innate Life Purpose).

- How you are to *be* as you go about fulfilling your Innate Purpose (your Innate Values).

- What you are to *use* as your primary resources as you go about fulfilling your Innate Life Purpose (your Innate Gifts).

"human nature" – That which you acquire as a human being from your personal experiences and from your worldly influences. All of your beliefs and attitudes were formed and/or acquired after you were born. Your beliefs and attitudes are of this physical world and do not have their roots in your Divine Source.

"Positively Brilliant Self" – The coexistence of your Divine Nature and human nature. Clarity, direction and resourcefulness are available from your Divine Nature. Your beliefs and attitudes are the realm of your human nature. When your human nature is in alignment with and is fully expressing your Divine Nature you are being your Positively Brilliant Self.

"Positively Brilliant Self-mastery" – The process of knowing, living, and celebrating your Positively Brilliant Self.

"operating beliefs" – All beliefs are operating beliefs that act as the underlying code directing your thinking, planning, behavior, actions, and goals.

"life-limiting beliefs and attitudes" – All beliefs and attitudes that hinder your full exploration, expression, or celebration of your Positively Brilliant Self.

"life-affirming beliefs and attitudes" – All beliefs and attitudes that enhance your full exploration, expression, or celebration of your Positively Brilliant Self.

"Innate" – Something that comes from your Divine Source.

"values" – Those adopted qualities that define the way you are as you do.

"Innate Values" – Those qualities that you are here to model to your world as you fulfill your Innate Life Purpose. Your first endowment from your Divine Source.

"life purpose" – What you have been told, or adopted unconsciously, that you should contribute to your world—family, community, organizations.

"Innate Life Purpose" – What you are uniquely qualified and Divinely imprinted to contribute to or serve your world—family, community, organizations. Your second endowment from your Divine Source.

"talents" – The learned skills and knowledge that you have developed that are not your Innate Gifts. Others often suggest or even insist that you develop specific skills or knowledge so you are prepared to be successful. That is successful as others define success.

These learned talents are not your natural strengths. Nor do these learned talents have their roots in your Divine Nature.

"Innate Gifts" – Your God-given skills, knowledge, and personal capacities that you were endowed with at birth. Your third endowment from your Divine Source. Your Innate Gifts serve as your primary resources to fulfill your Innate Life Purpose. They are and will always be within you. It is up to you to develop these to their full human potential.

"adopted" – The process by which you acquired beliefs and attitudes that do not support knowing, living and celebrating your Positively Brilliant Self.

The process by which you acquired others' values, purpose and talents that do not reflect your Divine Nature. Adoption can happen consciously and unconsciously.

<u>"conscious"</u> – The act of knowing what is taking place in the present moment. The opportunity to choose, or not choose for yourself.

SECTION I

Your Infinite Divine Nature

Remember this.
When people choose to withdraw far from a fire, the fire
continues to give warmth, but they grow cold.
When people choose to withdraw far from light, the light
continues to be bright in itself, but they are in darkness.
This is also the case when people withdraw from God.

—Augustine

In Section I, <u>Your Infinite Divine Nature</u>, we explore our Divine Nature and how it supports and informs who we are.

You are connected with a Divine Source that provides you with three endowments that make up your Divine Nature and because you are a human being you have a human nature.

Your Divine Nature is made up of three endowments, your unique Innate Values, an Innate Life Purpose, and Innate Gifts. Your Divine Source is directly accessible for Divine guidance.

Divine guidance is the most empowering, powerful, and aligned guidance that will ever be available to you during your life.

When your Divine Nature is authentically and fully expressed through your humanity, you experience bliss, fulfillment, and Positively Brilliant Self-mastery.

SECTION I EXPLORES THE FOLLOWING QUESTIONS:

1. What benefits come from a connection with your Divine Source?
2. How is your Divine Nature expressed through you?

Principle 1

✧ You are connected to an infinite and life-affirming Divine Source.

> *We are all spiritual beings having a human experience.*
> —Anonymous

I have always been connected to an infinite and life-affirming Divine Source even when I was too busy to remember. There are many names for the Divine: God, Spirit, Higher Power, Infinite Intelligence, Christ, Creator, and many more.

I am also living a very human life in a physical, three-dimensional world. As a human, I can get caught up in the worldly turmoil of duality, comparison, and ego. I have been encouraged to 'just do it,' and 'gut it out,' and 'do what I am told.' It is easy to understand why most people forget who they are and to what they are connected.

I forgot I am a Spiritual being having a human experience. My physical and hectic life drowned out the quiet voice of my Divine Source for the first 35 years of my life. I was busy doing and achieving and striving for more of what this world had to offer, such as money, power, recognition, influence, and position. There was no time to listen for or connect with anything that wasn't of this physical world.

For me, it took being aware and accepting three truths about myself and my life before I could open up to the possibility and desperate hope that there was a "Divine Something" and that I may be connected to It in some way.

1. <u>My way of working wasn't working</u> A realization that I could not keep up the same pace in my professional life any longer.

2. <u>My way of living had no life to it</u> A realization that I did not have a personal life or perhaps better stated as, the personal life I did have was devoid of any form of real intimacy.

3. <u>My Self-worth was bankrupt</u> I had a feeling of a growing emptiness and self-loathing deep inside. I had no idea who I really was.

Through a conscious decision, I decided I was going to get on my knees and pray every night before getting into bed and every morning when I got up.

This was a radically new behavior for me. The last time I remembered being on my knees praying was in a church nearly two decades earlier when I was at a Sunday mass. And even then it was more of a learned habit than a feeling of connecting with what I now would know as my Divine Source.

When I started, I was not sure what I was going to pray for or who exactly I was praying to. I initially needed to have blind faith in order to eventually know there was a Divine Source and I could gain a personal connection to that Divine Source.

My morning prayer was, "*Dear God, I am loving and lovable. I am self-worthy and self-caring. I am doing my best today. Bless my family and bless me.*" My evening prayer was, "*Dear God, today I did my best to be loving and lovable. I was self-worthy and self-caring. Bless my family and bless me.*"

Gradually, I began to have a relationship with what I now know as an infinite and life-affirming Divine Source. The endowments that come from my Divine Source make up my Divine Nature.

I have developed a daily Spiritual practice to connect to, dialog with, and open to receive my Divine Source's life-affirming guidance. My life has become more congruent and more meaningful as a direct result of my Spiritual practice.

When I follow my Divine Source's guidance, there is an easy and graceful unfolding. When I think my way into following my ego's guidance, it feels like I am forcing it, which is exactly what I am doing.

With practice, I have become better able to distinguish Divine's guidance from my ego's guidance.

A JOURNEY BACK TO YOUR POSITIVELY BRILLIANT SELF

- What do you call your Divine Source?
- How do you connect to your Divine Source?

- When and how often do you connect to your Divine Source?

- In what area of your life right now can you use guidance from your life-affirming Divine Source?

Principle 1: In Her Own Words

✧ You are connected to an infinite and life-affirming Divine Source.

"I Heard Myself Say . . ."

Ann Ranson

Dallas, TX

Inspired Business Models

www.annranson.com

For years, I have felt a strong connection to God. That connection has taken on a much deeper meaning in recent years.

I used to think that I was in control. I thought of myself as spiritual, yet I was also clear that I had power. After all, I was successful in business, had strong family and friend relationships—so I wasn't doing such a bad job now, was I?

All of that changed at the turn of the millennium. A coincidence? And so the changes began. First was a revelation that came as I was reading Who Moved My Cheese. *As I read "what would you do if you weren't afraid?," I heard a voice say, "Quit your job and move to DC." I was certain that something was broken inside me as there was no one in the room—yet the voice was as real as any I had heard. Next, I heard myself say to my son, "Let's move," a rare occurrence for a native Texan.*

Thus began my path of hearing myself say many life-changing things! After living in the DC area for more than four years, I again heard myself say, "Let's move back to Texas." This was totally unexpected, yet there we were packing again. During the process of saying goodbye to a friend, I heard myself say, "Would you like for me to coach you?" She replied enthusiastically, "YES!" What had I just said? I had a full-time job as a sales and marketing professional.

This simple question led me to a total career change, becoming a professional coach and public speaker. Many times since, I have heard myself say things that I know are sourced from God. My connection is constant and strong. Now I'm not surprised when "I hear myself say," as I know that God is once again leading me to a place I couldn't have imagined on my own.

Principle 2

✦ Your Divine Nature is infinitely resourceful, whole, and complete.

I am healthy, whole, and complete
In the infinity of life where I am,
all is perfect, whole, and complete.
I recognize my body as a good friend.
Each cell in my body has Divine Intelligence.
I listen to what it tells me,
and know that its advice is valid.
I am always safe, and
Divinely protected and guided.
I choose to be healthy and free.
All is well in my world.
—Louise Hay

There is nothing in my Divine Nature that is lacking or that needs to be fixed.

My Divine Nature forms an inner core of perfection. This is called in varying spiritual traditions a Soul, a Divine Spark, Christ Consciousness, or an Essential Self.

My Divine Nature is infinitely resourceful. For many, this comes through as an inner voice, or a calling. Others sense a knowing urge or a guiding force that continues to nudge them toward what best serves them and their life purpose. When you follow this inner voice or guiding force, you are in total alignment with your Positively Brilliant Self.

My Divine Nature is whole and connected to all that is. There is no separation. There is perfection in my Divine Nature that can never be taken away from me.

In this perfection, my Divine Nature is complete. There is nothing that needs to be added; no growth, no learning, no development or evolution is necessary. And there is nothing that needs to be taken away. My Divine Nature is perfectly healthy and even maintains the perfect weight. My Divine Nature has the perfect gifts, wisdom, and guidance to carry out its life's purpose.

I used to think if I accepted the idea that I am perfect, whole, and complete I would become lazy or not want to improve or learn more. The opposite has been true for me. Opening up to the perfection and guidance of my Divine Nature has allowed a fuller and more satisfying expression through my human nature.

Because my human nature is less than perfect, not quite complete, has limited resourcefulness and OK, is a bit over weight, accessing my Divine Nature is both practical and necessary. My Divine Nature has always been with me, but I have not always been connected to my Divine Nature. This is the importance of having a daily Spiritual practice so my humanness can remember to tap into the enormous benefits my Divine Nature offers.

I do not believe my Divine Nature changes over my lifetime. What I have experienced, however, is that my use of, access to, and understanding of my Divine Nature continue to evolve and deepen.

Your Divine Nature is the ultimate resource you will have during your lifetime. Your Divine Nature provides the ultimate foundation for you to know and be your Positively Brilliant Self.

A JOURNEY BACK TO YOUR POSITIVELY BRILLIANT SELF

- How is your Divine Nature:
    —Resourceful?
    —Whole?
    —Complete?
- When and where in your life have you experienced your Divine Nature as infinitely resourceful, whole, and complete?
- How has your Divine Nature been expressing Itself through your human nature?
- How could you benefit from your Divine Nature that is resourceful, whole, and complete?

Principle 2: In His Own Words

✦ Your Divine Nature is infinitely resourceful, whole, and complete.

Problems or Gifts?

Scott Bogart, Author and Life Coach
Ventura, CA

I would ask myself, "Why do I seem to be the only one who has these problems?" Okay, maybe I did notice that other people had a few things to deal with, too. But others' problems always appeared small in comparison.

It seemed that nothing was easy. Everything from getting up in the morning to getting to school on time presented challenges. Then there were the decisions: How am I going to make a living? How am I going to create the kind of life that will make me satisfied and that will be meaningful?

But then some interesting questions came to me. What if everything were exactly as I wanted it? What if no matter what I wanted I could have it instantly? At first, I drifted off into the fantasy of eating sweets, going to amusement parks, and being with lovely companions. But as I journeyed further into the fantasy, I came to realize that if things were this easy, life would ultimately become extremely boring. There would be no problems and no challenges to resourcefully face and from which to learn and grow.

My Divine Nature is indeed resourceful, whole, and complete. In this completeness, and in conjunction with my Divine connection to the Source, I have come to understand that my world is perfect in all of its seeming imperfections. It is only through these imperfections that I am given the opportunity to learn and to grow.

Now I fully understand that every problem and challenge that I face are co-creations between the Source and me. When presented with such challenges, I no longer allow myself to go to a space of frustration and angst. Instead, I just relax and give thanks for the manifestation. I put my faith into the resourcefulness, wholeness, and completeness of myself, and direct my thoughts toward what I'm meant to learn from the problem. I gracefully move through it and ultimately closer to the Source.

Principle 3:

✧ You have direct access to your Divine Source any time you choose.

I have so much to do today,
I'll need to spend another hour
on my knees praying.
—Martin Luther (1483–1546)

Yes, I actually do have direct access to my Divine Source. And so do you. How great is this?

This means I do not have to go through anyone else. I do not have to access my Divine Source through an institution or holy book. While an institution and holy writings may assist in reconnecting with your Divine Source, as well as provide support structures to remind you of your connection with the Divine, they are not mandatory for your direct access.

What makes direct access so important is you have the most powerful, infinite, and aligned resource available on a 24/7 basis. The realization I am having as I write this is how often I forget to tap into this, my most powerful and practical guiding resource.

When I am beginning a project or deciding on which path to follow, I access my Divine Source for guidance. When I am presented an opportunity to write, speak, or contribute my time or talents, I access my Divine Source for guidance.

How do I access my Divine Source?

Accessing my Divine Source for guidance is as simple as making a cell phone call. I set aside whatever I am doing, I quiet my mind with a few deep breaths, and I call upon my Divine Source for the guidance that will most support me right now. This can take one minute and generally does not exceed 10 minutes. I do not sit or breathe in any formal way. Most of the time spent is for me to clear my mind.

For the last several years, upon awakening I lay in bed in an alert sleep for up to 30 minutes. I call this my horizontal meditation. This morning meditation facilitates a Divine downloading process that has a purity of purpose and a just-in-time practicality.

Now, I hasten to add, the guidance that my Divine Source provides is not always what I want to 'hear' or embrace. In many cases, the guidance I receive has nothing to do with the question I asked. Well, at least it doesn't seem to have anything to do with the issue I am struggling with. So, of course, I'll ignore it, or when I'm feeling feisty, I'll argue that this guidance was obviously meant for someone else. If I am in a charitable mood, I'll even offer my Divine Source to deliver the guidance to the one who was meant to get it.

The cost of being defiant

These deflective strategies to not follow my Divine Source's guidance, by the way, have never worked. But I still give myself full permission to be defiant. So sometimes I will "just do it" or "make it happen." More and more, I realize that when I do "make it happen" a cost has been exacted.

This cost for me has been in the form of physical exhaustion, the realization of squandering my precious time, and, worst of all, adding nothing to my sense of personal fulfillment or Self-mastery.

When the guidance coming through seems so outrageous, I will write it down because it is hard for me to recall it even later that same day. The way that I perceive myself, my current willingness, and my personal capacities create a huge disconnect between what my Divine Source knows I am ready for and what my human nature thinks I'm ready for. Again, I give myself permission to not jump into the action of doing, proceeding, or implementing what my Divine Source has revealed to me.

During my 'now fruitless' protests and deflection strategies, I open myself to the possibilities, lessons, learning, support, signs, and people who begin to coalesce around what my Divine Source has revealed to me as part of my life's journey and purpose. When I have completed my stages of preparation to be ready and willing, I begin to align my human nature with my Divine Nature to physically manifest that which came from my Divine Source's guidance.

My experience continues to get reinforced when
I follow my Divine Source's guidance. I am always filled
with a deep sense of fulfillment. I am being my full,
authentic, magnificent, and Positively Brilliant Self.

A Journey Back to Your Positively Brilliant Self

- Have you called upon your Divine Source today?
- What issue, decision, or path could benefit
  from your Divine Source's guidance right now?

Principle 3: In Her Own Words

✦ You have direct access to your Divine Source any time you choose.

I Choose Now…and Now…and Now…

> LeAnn Riley, Realtor and Master Coach
> Minneapolis, MN
> www.affluentchoice.com

I was trying hard to rewrite my life through an opposi-tional divorce. I needed to connect with my Divine Source so I could feel better fast. Where was It? Who was I? How had this happened to me? I had lost myself in the mess and stress. I didn't want to go through this alone. Every day was tough, caring for the kids alone and running a business I owned with my soon-to-be ex-spouse. I was miserable and needed help. Where was I going to live?

A few years before, I had reconnected and began going to church. This forced me to meet people and cre-ate a new spirit-based community. That wasn't enough, I wanted more connection. I began a practice of closing my eyes each morning upon waking and praying for healing and closeness. Sometimes I even asked for some help. I began to meditate regularly.

Then I realized a few things about my Divine Source. I was responsible for myself and two children.

*Who did I know best to get me through this? In a moment of clarity, I realized **I, LeAnn, am my own Divine Source. I choose to know Myself fully and trust in My Gifts.***

I began to focus on my courage and tenacity. I listed my greatest characteristics. I was operating with an innate sense of determination. I knew, deep down inside, I am a survivor!

My Divine Source is who I am on the inside when all cylinders are firing. I learned to call forth my own Divine Self because she was the one who could help me. She had faith and trust and would never let me down, no matter what.

I began to sort out what I could do each day, knowing I could also choose just to enjoy the moment as it is, good or bad. I got to choose from my own source. I can choose Now…and Now…and so I keep asking myself, "What does my Divine Source say Now?"

SECTION II

Your Creative Human Nature
Life-affirming beliefs and attitudes

Success is peace of mind which is a direct result of self-satisfaction in knowing you did your best to become the best you are capable of becoming.
—John R. Wooden

In Section II, <u>Your Creative Human Nature</u>, we explore how our human nature assimilates beliefs and attitudes.

Our human nature is also our vehicle of expression for our Divine Nature's Innate Values, Innate Life Purpose, and Innate Gifts.

We explore our Innate Values in Section III, chapters 10, 11, 12, and 13.

We explore our Innate Life Purpose in Section IV, chapters 14, 15, 16, and 17.

We explore our Innate Gifts in Section V, chapters 18, 19, 20, and 21.

Our beliefs and attitudes

Our beliefs and attitudes are acquired from and reinforced by our personal experiences and by our worldly influences.

All of my beliefs and attitudes were formed and/or acquired upon entering the human realm. My beliefs and attitudes are of this physical world and do not have their roots in my Divine Nature.

My beliefs and attitudes are of this physical world and do not have their roots in my Divine Nature.

My parents and schooling contributed to what I absorbed or adopted as my primary beliefs and attitudes.

Nearly all early beliefs and attitudes are assimilated unconsciously. When I was young, these beliefs and attitudes certainly made sense within the context of what others told me how life is supposed to be lived.

Now that I am a mostly conscious adult and mostly over the need to please others, I can examine my beliefs and attitudes to determine if they support the expression of my Innate Life Purpose.

When my beliefs and attitudes do support me, I celebrate them.

When my beliefs and attitudes do not support me to fully express my Innate Life Purpose, I change them.

Can I change a belief I have had my whole life? Absolutely! This realization was a life-changing event for me when I was about 35 years old.

Life-affirming beliefs

When I came to realize that my beliefs, while deeply ingrained, were only deeply ingrained because I had reinforced these beliefs for 35 years, I now had the choice and ability to change them.

I was now free from the tyranny and hopelessness that I would always be at the mercy of beliefs that no longer served me or my life's work. Life-affirming beliefs are explored in chapters 4, 5, and 6.

Life-affirming attitudes

My attitudes are a choice I make every moment. My attitudes can be life-affirming in a manner that supports me to live a life of purpose.

Or I can live with attitudes that undermine living my life in a congruent state with my most authentic Self. The choice here is accomplished either consciously or unconsciously. Life-affirming attitudes are explored in chapters 7, 8, and 9.

SECTION II EXPLORES THE FOLLOWING QUESTIONS:

1. What are your current beliefs and attitudes?
2. Do they continue to serve you?
3. What beliefs and attitudes would you like to change?
4. What beliefs and attitudes would better serve you and your Innate Life Purpose?
5. What beliefs and attitudes best support you in knowing, living, and celebrating your Positively Brilliant Self?
6. How can you change your beliefs and attitudes?

Principle 4

A LIFE-AFFIRMING BELIEF

✧ You believe that when you are connected to and guided by your sense of the Divine you are infinitely resourceful.

> *Resolve to be thyself: and*
> *know, that he who finds himself,*
> *loses his misery.*
> —Matthew Arnold

All my beliefs are the domain of my human nature. When I was born, I did not come into this physical world with any beliefs. They are all acquired from my human environment and experiences.

My beliefs about the existence of a Divine Source, and if there is a Divine, what my connection to It is, came from human influences.

My cultural history, passed down from generation to generation, held beliefs that God is all powerful and has very strict and unbendable rules on acceptable and unacceptable behaviors that would direct me to heaven or hell. I had a fear of God. Yes, I would pray to God for forgiveness and 'favors,' but I cannot remember ever going to my God for practical, everyday guidance.

My beliefs have also come from how I interpret my own Spiritual experiences. Nearly all of my early beliefs were acquired unconsciously and went unexamined for more than 35 years.

All my beliefs are continuously being reinforced by whom and with what I surround myself. I now believe through my own direct experiences that when I am connected to and guided by my Divine Source I have an infinite resourcefulness that guides my life's choices, my purpose, and my life's work.

A JOURNEY BACK TO YOUR POSITIVELY BRILLIANT SELF

- Do the beliefs about your connection with your Divine Source support you to live your most Positively Brilliant Self?

   —If so, celebrate!

   —If not, are you ready to change the belief?
- What belief about your Divine Source would bring an infinite resourcefulness into your life?
- Who are the people around you who support your belief in an infinitely resourceful Divine?

Principle 4: In Her Own Words

A LIFE-AFFIRMING BELIEF

✧ You believe that when you are connected to and guided by your sense of the Divine you are infinitely resourceful.

Becoming Spaciousness

Jennifer Sellers, CEO, Coach

Inspired Mastery

Tucson, AZ

www.inspiredmastery.com

On some level, I always knew I was a part of something much larger than myself. I remember walking in puddles after a rainstorm and seeing the sky and clouds reflected in them. It felt like I was walking on the sky. I was thrilled and frightened, and immersed in pure awe.

As I grew older, the connection wasn't so much there. As long as things were going well in my life, it didn't much matter. But when they didn't, there was nothing for me to rely on . . . nothing for me to take refuge in other than my intellect and my ability to solve problems.

Because I had no connection to the vastness, to pure potentiality, to my Higher Self, I was filled with anxiety, and what's worse, I was hiding that fact from myself. Life was a problem to be solved, and while I was great at solving one problem after another, I hadn't a clue about how to solve Life itself. It was hopeless, I was hopeless, and there was nothing I could do about any of it.

I was very competent at what I did, I was sensitive and intuitive, I was caring and cared for, I was loving and loved. But I didn't have access to the beauty of my own life.

Over time, I've been able to access the Divine presence and the sparkling "thusness" of life.

I am spaciousness. I inspire conscious awareness. My mission is to move all of us to act out of compassion for ourselves and others.

When I first went to a therapist in my early 30s, I was surprised to receive test results that said I was anxious. But knowing that truth was a first step toward my now truth: that I am an extension of the Divine, as we all are. I now feel more peace than anxiety, more excitement than fear, more love for myself than doubt. And when the anxiety, fear, and doubt visit, I eventually—not always right away!—know to welcome them, learn from them, and allow them their say. They, too, are Divine Guidance.

$\mathcal{P}$rinciple 5

A LIFE-AFFIRMING BELIEF

✧ You believe that when you bring your Innate Gifts to your Innate Life Purpose as you honor your Innate Values you are living your Positively Brilliant Self.

> *When I discover who I am,*
> *I'll be free.*
> —Ralph Ellison

This belief has been a guiding belief for the work I have consciously been engaged in for the past two decades. It has been important to me to bring my human nature and my Divine Nature together in a way that is simple, understandable, and practical.

This belief has proved to be a guiding foundation for living my own life and supporting more than a thousand helping professionals who have in turn helped tens of thousands of other people to move toward their Positively Brilliant Self-mastery.

By believing this belief, I have had the experience of transcending the limitations of past programming, mass consciousness, and current circumstances. My Divine Nature, (my Innate Values, Innate Life Purpose, and Innate Gifts) can now guide my plans, strategies, decisions, and actions back to my most authentic Self.

This foundational belief is simple to understand.

    A. Your Divine Source endows your Divine Nature with a unique combination of Innate Values, an Innate Life Purpose, and Innate Gifts.

    B. Your human nature's job is to know, live, and celebrate each endowment within your Divine Nature.

This foundational belief is practical for everyday decisions, plans, and actions. Once you have discovered and articulated your Innate Values, Life Purpose, and Gifts, you now have the ability to align your day-to-day personal and professional life with your most authentic and Positively Brilliant Self.

A Journey Back to Your Positively Brilliant Self

- Do you believe that you have the opportunity to live your own life?
- Do you know, live, and celebrate your Divine Nature (your Innate Values, Purpose, and Gifts) as expressed through your human nature?
- What evidence do you already have in your life that at least part of your life is your own life?

Principle 5: In Her Own Words

A LIFE-AFFIRMING BELIEF

✧ You believe that when you bring your Innate Gifts to your Innate Life Purpose as you honor your Innate Values you are living your Positively Brilliant Self.

Can I Be Myself Already?

Phyliss Francis, PCC, Professional Certified
Coach, Speaker
Honolulu, HI
www.awakeninglives.com

I remember my father telling me, "You have to be the best at everything you do to succeed in this world because you have two strikes against you: you are black and you are a woman." I bought into the belief that my core value was to represent my race and gender, and make my family proud.

While I was growing up, this belief was perpetuated by living in upper-class neighborhoods and attending private Catholic schools that lacked diversity. I remember being told, "You're special because you're not like other black people," and this was intended to be a compliment. I spent most of my life trying to fit into a mold that I believed my environment expected.

Growing up with this underlying belief made it difficult for me to recognize my natural gifts and talents. I could not distinguish my personal values and authentic self-expression from others' expectations. I tried to fit in socially and professionally by being perfect so that people would see beyond my two "strikes" and get my worth. After receiving two degrees, acquiring multiple certifications, earning promotions and awards, it was no surprise that I was left feeling exhausted and unsatisfied. I recognized that my insatiable appetite to achieve was fueled by underlying feelings of unworthiness.

When I was supported to focus on the positive, and encouraged to allow my authentic Self to emerge, I felt my self-perception shift from judgment to acknowledgment. I changed my focus from what is wrong and needs to be fixed, to what is working, what is the lesson, and self-acceptance.

I discovered my core values and learned to align them with my daily actions. I discovered my life's purpose statement: **I am whole, perfect, and complete in this moment! All that I need is within me as I shine my transforming light into the world.**

Now, I effortlessly express my authentic Self in everything I do. I am a beautiful black woman who has value simply because I breathe. I am attracting diverse professional projects that use my natural gifts and talents. I am experiencing more joy and fulfillment than ever.

Principle 6

A LIFE-AFFIRMING BELIEF

✧ You believe that when you acknowledge yourself for living your own life you are reenergized to contribute even more of you to your world.

Nothing splendid has ever been achieved except by those who dared believe that something inside them was superior to circumstance.
—Bruce Barton

To acknowledge myself for living my own life, several factors have to be in place.

1. I had to first know my authentic Self.
2. I aligned a life choice with my authentic Self.
3. I had to be aware enough to notice that this particular life choice supported me to be living my own life.
4. I made the connection between making this life-affirming choice and how good it felt deep down inside my being.
5. I took time to acknowledge myself for making this life-affirming choice.
6. I fully opened to receive my own acknowledgment with a deep sense of gratitude.

There are two great benefits once you have the competence to accomplish all six steps and can consciously repeat this process. First, you reinforce how good it feels to be living your own life. Second, you generate a surge of energy and strengthen being your Innate Values, living your Innate Life Purpose, and using your Innate Gifts.

Your world is desperate to have more of you. Not the pre-molded-by-others-you but the Positively Brilliant one-and-only-authentic-you.

You are the only person who can make your unique contribution to your world. The only way you make your full and unique contribution to your world is when your most authentic Self is living your own life.

While beliefs are formed as part of your human nature, embodying this belief allows you to experience and contribute more of your Divine Nature.

A Journey Back to Your Positively Brilliant Self

- Acknowledge every life-affirming choice you make that is congruent with your Positively Brilliant Self.
- Feel the surge of vitality and renewal to be even more of your Positively Brilliant Self.

Principle 6: In His Own Words

A LIFE-AFFIRMING BELIEF

✧ You believe that when you acknowledge yourself for living your own life you are reenergized to contribute even more of you to your world.

How My Fallback Plan Sabotaged My Authenticity

Steve Dimmick, Mentor to Passionate
Entrepreneurs
Fort Collins, CO
www.AwakeningInsight.com

"One of these days I'm going to start doing what I really want to do, but first I need to make some money." This is what I told myself for nearly two years. The problem was I wasn't making any money, I was stressed out, and I didn't feel authentic at all.

I kept trying different business ideas. I wanted to succeed at something, something other than what I really wanted to do. I thought that earning money at something else first would alleviate the pressure of succeeding at what my heart yearned to do.

By keeping my desired contribution to the world as my backup plan, I kept myself in a state of continual struggle.

On the verge of financial collapse, I was finally forced to acknowledge my deep-felt desires and recognize my full authentic Self. I realized the fear of success was keeping my Positively Brilliant contribution forever as my back-up plan.

I started sharing my values of service and clarity to help others express their passions. I became conscious of my innate ability to help others expand their visions even more.

I am energized by my own unique and authentic Self to contribute to the success of other passionate entrepreneurs in the pursuit of their visions.

I am now actively engaged in helping service-based entrepreneurs go from passions to profit, while at the same time living my life purpose of teaching, mentoring, and guiding others on their life's journey.

Now that I am expressing my authentic Self every day, I am experiencing a vitality and energy I have never known before. By acknowledging my Positively Brilliant Self, I am living a life of fulfillment and authenticity.

$\mathcal{P}$rinciple 7

A LIFE-AFFIRMING ATTITUDE

✦ You love and accept who you are right now.

> *The greatest discovery of my generation is that*
> *human beings can alter their lives by altering*
> *their attitudes of mind.*
> —William James

This is my current definition of life mastery—*I love and accept who I am right now.* Can you imagine living in the consistent attitude that you love and accept yourself in this moment, and now in this moment, and...? Well, you get the idea.

Maintaining this attitude has been fleeting for me; it comes and goes. I have noticed this attitude is vulnerable to the caustic environments around me (and, for that matter, within my own critical mind) that reinforce '*I'm not enough yet,*' or '*I should be aspiring to...,*' or '*I'll be more lovable when . . .*'

I suspect I will be practicing the art of returning to this attitude for the rest of my life. Or perhaps I could embrace the idea that I will not be in the perpetual mindset of 'I love and accept who I am right now' and just go ahead and 'love and accept who I am right now...even when I am not loving and accepting who I am right now.' Now that's a life-affirming attitude with attitude.

I am human

I embrace that I am perfectly imperfect. I make mistakes. I forget who I really am. I lose track of my values, purpose, and gifts. Big deal! Welcome to the human experience.

I have an insatiable curiosity. I love to learn, grow, explore, and evolve. I am fascinated by the world I live in. I laugh and cry as I connect with people I have never met when I hear or see their stories. Yes, this, too, is part of the human experience.

When I fully experience this attitude of 'I love and accept who I am right now,' I absorb the fullness of my life. I literally increase my capacity to love and accept myself every time I bring this attitude into my mind and body.

A JOURNEY BACK TO YOUR POSITIVELY BRILLIANT SELF

- Create a reminder for yourself, perhaps a note for your bathroom mirror.
- What is there to love and accept about you now?
- How are you going to bring this life-affirming attitude into your own life?

Principle 7: In His Own Words

A LIFE-AFFIRMING ATTITUDE

✧ You love and accept who you are right now.

Am I Too Different to Be Loved?

Marc A. Carignan, President & CEO

Life Success Strategies, Inc.

San Diego, CA

www.lifesuccessstrategies.com

"What if somebody really gets to know me? Will people I love still love me if they know the 'real me'?" Thoughts like these used to run through my mind every day, as I continually doubted who I was, what I was worth, and where I would be allowed to go in life. And the answer to the 'real me' question in my mind was always 'no.'

I knew I was different from other children. I thought this difference, which I couldn't really describe at the time, was something unusual. In my teens, I discovered the difference that I had felt deep inside years before. Due to my strict religious upbringing, I could not share this knowledge with my friends and family. I had already received the word on the topic from my Church. What was that discovery? That I was a gay man.

The biggest problem about being gay was not the comments, intolerance, and lack of understanding from others but those same negative thoughts about myself that I had internalized, an inner homophobia that was running rampant in my mind and in my heart. I was living in pain and fear, thinking and feeling it every day. I was overcome with fear: fear of not belonging, of being alone, but mostly fear of not being loved or even lovable.

It didn't take long for me to turn to food as comfort. I became the fat kid in school. By high school, I had added alcohol to the mix. These substances allowed me to escape my negative feelings, at least for a while. And they became an addiction.

At the time, I had no idea that I could be a gay man and Positively Brilliant at the same time! My change of heart started by releasing this negative self-talk as not the truth but simply some people's opinions. Little by little, I began to see myself as a person worthy of the same respect as any other person. Over time, this grew into the knowledge and acceptance of my fuller Self and that I had a unique set of gifts, talents, and purpose. I starting believing that I was truly a magnificent expression of the Divine.

I am a courageous, loving, magnificent man who celebrates his Divinity, authentically and joyously creating an environment that allows others to acknowledge and celebrate their Divinity as well.

I now consciously live each day in gratitude, starting each morning with time to reflect on the appreciation I have for my life and the way that I am: beautiful, magnificent, and gay. I focus on the positives in life, look for the best in others, and am patient with myself when I don't perform to my highest potential. I am now attracting more wealth, health, and amazing relationships in my life, including a beautiful, passionate man I now love.

Fear still creeps in, but my conscious awareness of it allows me to change my thinking and focus on the truth that I am perfect just the way I am right now. When I focus on this truth, coming from a place of love, acceptance, and trust, there is no longer any room for fear. All I need to do is remember the truth.

Principle 8

A Life-Affirming Attitude

✦ You take responsibility for creating your life.

> *Our lives are not determined by...what life*
> *brings to us, but by the attitude we bring to life.*
> *A positive attitude causes a chain reaction of positive*
> *thoughts, events, and outcomes. It is a catalyst, a spark*
> *that creates extraordinary results.*
>
> —Anonymous

What a great attitude this is. By taking on this attitude, you will in a single stroke stop being a victim and stop being at the mercy of what others think you should do or how you should be.

It is a call to be responsible for living your own life and for creating what aligns with your most authentic Self. This is a life-liberating attitude.

This completely reorients your thinking and focus to start looking for and choosing what best serves you to be living your own life. The 'you' that is being served is your Positively Brilliant you, your Divine you. Not the old you who has been living someone else's life.

For the first 37 years of my life, other people pretty much 'created my life.' I was on auto-pilot with an attitude that I had to do and be what others wanted. This burned me out. When I changed my attitude to create my own life, I reclaimed my life forever.

You are the only one who can take responsibility for creating your own life. And you have a choice as to what life you are living: one of Self-mastery or other-directed-mastery.

A Journey Back to Your Positively Brilliant Self

- Notice when you are and when you are not taking responsibility for creating your own life.
- When you are not taking responsibility for creating your own life, who is creating your life for you?
- How responsible are you for creating your current life?
- Are there any parts of your life you are ready to take more responsibility for creating?
- When you choose the attitude of taking responsibility for your own life, what type of life are you taking responsibility for?

Principle 8: In Her Own Words

A LIFE-AFFIRMING ATTITUDE

✧ You take responsibility for creating your life.

It All Comes Down to Me!

> Sheri Boone, MCC, CLC
> Inspired Mastery
> Portland, OR
> www.inspiredmastery.com
> www.mccmentorcoach.com

Twenty-three years ago, life was hard. My work was unsatisfying, my husband was suffering at his job, and it seemed that other people were directing my life. I was unhappy.

One fall day, I decided to take myself for a walk around my living room. On a deep intuitive level, I sensed that I could make a new choice for myself. That day, as I chose to be receptive and open to new possibilities, an idea began to sprout and within hours had fully blossomed. A few months later, my family and I were headed to Kauai, Hawaii, to live for six months.

Some around us, well-meaning family and friends, were more than willing to share their opinions and advice about our choice to quit jobs, cash in 401(k)s, and take off to the islands. But, at the same time, there was another group who was very supportive of our decision. For me, once I had my plan, nothing was going to deter me, and those opinions of others— positive or negative—were not even on my radar.

I had finally chosen to take responsibility for creating my life.

What freedom! As I moved ahead with all of the planning, organizing, and details of moving a family of four away from our home to an island life, I began to feel and live the joyous experience of living "at choice." I knew that whatever the outcome of this decision, I was making it happen. I was willing to take full responsibility for this choice, happily and fully.

From that day in my living room forward, I have never again doubted that my life is my job and my responsibility. It feels great, and oh, what a glorious life it is! As Joni Mitchell sings, "It all comes down to you." (I substitute 'me' of course!)

$Principle$ 9

A LIFE-AFFIRMING ATTITUDE

✧ You focus on the positive in yourself and others.

*Choosing to be positive and having a grateful attitude is
going to determine how you're going to live your life.*
—Joel Osteen

A positive focus opens up your mind to all the things in
your life that actually work. You begin to see all the
people, opportunities, natural gifts, beliefs and yes even
other attitudes that serve you. You begin to feel peace,
joy, happiness, and, yes, fulfillment. A positive focus
does not mean you bury your head in the sand.
With your head in the sand, you cannot see anything—
the positive or the negative.

Much of our world reinforces what is not working.
The media have a very crass saying: "if it bleeds, it
leads." The media collect all the accidents, wars, sensa-
tional scandals, riots, pending dangers, etc. and then
report them as the news of the day.

During this same day, millions of parents dressed,
fed, and hugged their beautiful children before getting
them to school. Millions of people performed acts of
compassion for their fellow humans. Billions of people
went about their day today, working, learning, praying,
caring, and playing. None of these life-affirming events
were reported on the evening news.

In school, our teachers point out what we got wrong, missed, or still need to learn. In work environments, employees are critiqued for what they did wrong. Again, billions of people learned something new today, or integrated or mastered a life-affirming skill into their personal or professional life. The sad part is what was being learned, integrated and mastered today was mostly ignored. When we are bombarded day after day with what is not working, or not yet mastered we begin to forget how spectacular and Positively Brilliant we are.

There is an unrealized resourcefulness that is available for those who look at their daily lives and recognize all of their beauty, love, and strength.

A Journey Back to Your Positively Brilliant Self

- What is working in your life today?
- What do you admire in those closest to you?
- What strengths in you are you focused on?
- What strengths in others are you focused on?

Principle 9: In His Own Words

A Life-Affirming Attitude

✧ You focus on the positive in yourself and others.

My Kids Are Smarter Than I Thought

Allen R. Valencour, Professional Certified Coach
CEO, Off Field Coaching, Inc.®
Prescott Valley, AZ
al@offfieldcoaching.com

Being a parent used to be a real challenge for me. I was caught between wanting to allow my children to make their own mistakes and wanting to protect them. I wanted them to learn their own lessons, and I wanted to tell them what to do because I knew better. And, as many parents do, I fell into the "because I said so" mentality of raising my children. It just seemed easier for me!

As a result, my children seldom felt heard and often felt limited with no good reason. As a parent, I felt constantly challenged by my kids. The only way I felt confident in my role as a father was by positioning myself as the "ultimate authority." It did not have the effect I had hoped for. My relationship with my kids was becoming increasingly strained.

When my daughter was 11 and my son 13, I attended a coach training school to become a professional life coach. One of the many things I learned was to focus on the positive within myself and others.

Upon returning home, I started to apply that Principle to my family and myself. All of a sudden, I could see that in many ways I was a great father and my children were great kids who were a lot smarter than I had given them credit for. **I began speaking from that positive place within me, and my children began hearing from that positive place within them.**

Rather than focusing on their faults (negatives), I focused on their strengths (positives). It completely transformed our relationship from one of struggle and adversity to one of cooperation, in which we all focused on our strengths.

After many years of implementing this Principle, I am delighted with the relationships my wife and I enjoy with our children. At 17 and 19, they are more responsible and mature than many "adults" I know. They openly share everything about their lives with us (the good and the not-so-good), knowing that we support them in all they do.

SECTION III

Being Your Innate Values

*Open your arms to change, but don't
let go of your values.*
—Dalai Lama

In Section III, <u>Being Your Innate Values</u>, you are guided toward knowing, living, and celebrating your Innate Values.

When I am being my Innate Values, I am being my Positively Brilliant Self.

Your Innate Values are inside you. They have been there since birth. They are there right now for you to uncover, nurture, develop, and use as your guide.

The untapped energy, clarity, and direction that are waiting for you to experience by *being your Innate Values* are life-changing. You begin to experience being yourself. You begin to experience a profound sense of alignment, centeredness, fulfillment, and inner peace.

Growing your capacity to care

By *being your Innate Values,* you begin to honor yourself and take better care of yourself. This point is really important because you are the only one who can take care of your innermost Positively Brilliant Self.

The paradox for those of us who are care-givers and have known a life of sacrifice, or "it's more important I take care of you first" mentality, is that by taking better care of ourselves we have a bigger capacity and more energy to give even more to those we love.

SECTION III EXPLORES THE FOLLOWING QUESTIONS:

1. What are your Innate Values?
2. Are your Innate Values different from the values you live by now?
3. How are your Innate Values used in living your Positively Brilliant Self-mastery?

Principle 10

✦ Your Innate Values are an endowment from your Divine Source.

Man's Search for meaning is the primary motivation in his life and not a 'secondary rationalization' of instinctual drives. This meaning is unique and specific in that it must and can be fulfilled by him alone; only then does it achieve a significance which will satisfy his own will to meaning… Man, however, is able to live and even to die for the sake of his ideals and values!
—Victor Frankl

Your Innate Values are your first endowment from your Divine Source. Your Innate Values are held as part of your Divine Nature.

Each of us embodies a unique set of Innate Values. These Innate Values are bestowed on us by our Divine Source. My unique set of Innate Values inspires me and defines my most authentic human beingness. My Innate Values are my deepest and strongest expression of my Divine Nature through the medium of my human nature.

During a significant part of my life, I did not know my own Innate Values. I followed only those values that I had unconsciously acquired from my childhood, formal schooling, and the organizations that I was a member. These were not bad values in and of themselves. The significant difference is these adopted values were not my most powerful, guiding, or fulfilling Innate Values.

I was very successful in obtaining the academic and goal-oriented accolades, as well the financial rewards, by following others' values. And it was exhausting and unfulfilling.

I discovered my own Innate Values by accessing my Divine Nature. I will discuss rediscovering, aligning, and celebrating my own Innate Values in my life in the next three Principles.

A Journey Back to Your Positively Brilliant Self

- What are your Innate Values?
- How does your Divine Nature express itself through your Innate Values?
- When you model a way of being that feels Divine, what value is present?

Principle 10: In Her Own Words

✧ Your Innate Values are an endowment from your Divine Source.

My Values Influence My Thoughts, Behaviors, and Actions

Marcy Johnsrude, Inspired Coach, Consultant, Trainer, Author, and Writer

Nanaimo, British Columbia

For many years, I tended to identify only with values related to work such as expediency and a good work ethic. I had no idea there could be different categories or origins of values, or the significance of this.

Then, about 10 years ago, during a Philosophy class discussion about morality, the whole concept came together for me. That discussion occurred a week after I was involved in a values exercise at work where our facilitator had asked, "If you had the ability to change a negative situation as a result of your core values, what would these core values be, what morals or values would you put your back up against the wall for?"

I had been struggling with so many questions about values, such as: Why did my values change when circumstances changed? Are there different types of values? Are values innate or learned? Are values and morals related? Suddenly, in the middle of that

Philosophy class, I knew that there are, indeed, different categories and origins of values. For example, my work and family values appear to be more situational or external, and while I find some of these values annoyingly persistent, I realize, now, that they are purely habitual and not necessarily related to my core values.

The big question is, Are my moral beliefs related to my core values, and are my core values innate? All I know is that I have certain core values that influence my present and subsequent thoughts and behaviors, For example, if I do something akin to my core values, there doesn't appear to be any negative consequences. On the other hand, if I act outside my core values, I often become frustrated or sad or whatever is pertinent to a particular situation. This leads me to believe that my core values of **integrity, justice, honesty, love, joy, and responsibility** are deeply rooted in me and, yes, they are innate.

There is no doubt in my mind that I was born with certain core values, and these values must have come from some universal source. I also believe that these values are what keep me true to myself and allow me to be the best that I can be for myself and others.

Principle 11

✦ You know your Innate Values.

I wanted to explore the values that are at work,
underpinning my life.
—Sidney Poitier

Innate Values represent the 'being' in human being. My Innate Values are the most authentic, joyous, and fulfilling way for me to be as a human being.

My Innate Values are **Creative, Connected, Thriving, Retreat, and Free to Express**. My adopted values from early life were *hard work, control, persistence,* and *serve others first*.

As I am busy doing the activities of my life, who am I being as I do my life? As I write this book, am I being *'creative'* or am I being *'controlling'*? The first Innate Value brings me joy; the second adopted value wears me out.

My adopted values are not bad values, in and of themselves. They just are not the most joyous, energetic, and fulfilling way for me to be my most authentic and Positively Brilliant Self.

Before you can live in alignment with your Innate Values, you have to know them. Every person has his or her own unique combination of Innate Values.

Examples of other Innate Values

Passion – Elegance – Ease – Love – Grace – Unity – Beauty – Centered – Humility – Healthy – Wisdom – Limitless – Exciting – Integrity – Natural – Joyous

Knowing your own unique combination of Innate Values is the first step toward Self-mastery that is inspired by your Divine Nature.

When you are able to access and articulate your Innate Values, you have the opportunity to replace any adopted values that do not serve your Self-mastery.

The next Principle will explore how to begin to align your life to honor your Innate Values.

A Journey Back to Your Positively Brilliant Self

- When you are in your happiest and most fulfilled moments, what qualities and way of being are you demonstrating?
- What are you most proud of in your way of being, at work, at home, or when you are alone?
- How is your Divine Nature best exemplified through your way of being?

Principle 11: In Her Own Words

✧ You know your Innate Values.

Memory's First Love

> Bonnie Leonard, EdD, CLC
> Midlife Coach for Women
> North Kingstown, RI
> www.bonnieleonard.com

On my way to becoming a life coach, I attended two excellent coach-training programs. Each featured a guided visualization to help elicit our core values. While both processes were impressive, the values that emerged in my Coach For Life (CFL) training rang so true, they are the ones I remember years later.

*My partner for the CFL exercise was especially helpful because she echoed my own words back to me, rather than changing them, even slightly, into her own. So, with her assistance, I discovered that my number one innate value is **Beauty of the Earth**.*

Before this experience, if someone had asked me whether this particular value was essential for me, I would have actually replied, "Yes." (I love to garden; my house is filled with potted ferns, sparkling crystals, smooth rocks, and sea-worn shells. Plus, I majored in geology as an undergraduate.) But no one talks about values with words like **Beauty of the Earth,** or the other core values I uncovered: **Open Connection, It's All Easy, Full Moon Rising, and Learning**.

Once I became aware of these fundamental values, I began to look back over my life and see how consistently the practice of honoring them had left me with a profound sense of fulfillment.

I even discovered that my earliest memory contained my top core value. At about eight months of age, I was lying outside under a tree in my kitty-coop (a small, screened, outdoor crib). The snippet of recall I have from that summer's day is the intoxicating scent of what I would later come to know as the smell of fresh-cut grass. This primal sensation of experiencing the **Beauty of the Earth** etched a groove in my psyche that remains to this day.

Currently, I live in a small, rented cottage on a cove, where I find myself adding a new garden every year. Does it make financial sense for me to invest time and money increasing the worth of someone else's property? Not really. Will this logic stop me? No. It's a matter of honoring an innate value and that always brings satisfaction and joy!

Principle 12

✧ You live in alignment with your Innate Values.

The world is full of people that have stopped listening to themselves or have listened only to their neighbors to learn what they ought to do, how they ought to behave, and what the values are they should be living for.

—Joseph Campbell

Now that you know your Innate Values, you have the opportunity to consciously live your own Innate Values.

The majority of my life was centered on doing. I was doing chores around the house, doing my schoolwork, and doing my job. I had created a tornado of doing. Along the way, I was rewarded with the label of "over-achiever." I was proud but, at the age of 35, exhausted. I told my friends I should be allowed to retire since I had done the equivalent of 20 years of study plus 50 years of work. And I felt 70 years old.

By living in alignment with my Innate Values of **Creative, Connected, Thriving, Retreat, and Free to Express,** I now teach, coach, and write about what you are reading right now. I could not have conceived of doing any of these before knowing and living in alignment with my own Innate Values.

Living my own Innate Values instead of living adopted values from other people means as decisions or planning comes up I can look at my Innate Values to determine which choice will most honor them.

Most people have lived the majority of their lives unconsciously following other people's values. Even when people successfully live aligned with other people's values, they experience emptiness inside.

Most people are not conscious about living through others' values. They cannot articulate this until months later when they have discovered their own Innate Values and have had the experience of honoring and aligning their own Innate Values in every part of their lives. Life becomes an easier flow and significantly more fulfilling.

A Journey Back to Your Positively Brilliant Self

- What decision are you dealing with today?
- How could your Innate Values be honored in what you decide?

Principle 12: In Her Own Words

✧ You live in alignment with your Innate Values.

My Life as an Old Typewriter

> Caryn McCurry, Inspirer of Choice
> New York, NY
> www.singularitynyc.com

One day I woke up, at the age of 42, and there they were: Dishes, Diapers, Laundry, Cleaning, Ding! Vshzzzhuup! (carriage return) Dishes, Diapers, Laundry, Cleaning, Ding! Vshzzzhuup! This was my life. And I said to myself, "So this is it!?"

By existing only in response to others, I had forgotten about me. For survival, I had sedated a part of who I was.

It was a piece of me so full of warmth and caring. It was the voice desperate to contribute that was screaming to be heard. It was the mind dulled from inactivity, too tired to think. Ding! Vshzzzhuup!

There seemed to be no room for me. Responsibilities to my family and home were all consuming. It seemed I was sinking. I had so much but felt so little. My days were filled with loneliness and resentment. I saw no choice. Ding! Vshzzzhuup!

One day, during a moment of anxiety and confusion, I experienced a threatening fear. Panicked, I pulled out my values, and sitting quietly, I read them over and over again. **My values are Love, Truth, Maternal, Vision, and Journey.**

And then I remembered I had had the answers all along. My truth was within, and by loving myself and nurturing what I have always known to be true, I found direction. I was free to begin my journey. I began to explore; my brain stretched from its long slumber and started to learn. I threw my arms back, took a deep breath, and started to grow.

Today I am preparing to launch my new business, Singularity. My purpose is to support other moms as they return to work. I encourage self-valuing and the discovery of choice. It is with a warm heart that I extend my hand.

I still have my old typewriter, but it is with cutting-edge technology that I embrace who I choose to be!

$\mathcal{P}$rinciple 13

✧ You acknowledge and celebrate living in alignment with your Innate Values.

We're so engaged in doing things to achieve purposes of outer value that we forget that the inner value, the rapture that is associated with being alive, is what it's all about.
—Joseph Campbell

This Principle completes the first cycle of your Self-mastery evolution. That is, knowing, living, and now celebrating the fact that you are living in alignment with your Innate Values. To be at this stage means you have discovered your Innate Values, lived in alignment with your Innate Values, and actually noticed when you have lived in alignment with your Innate Values in some part of your life. This is cause for great celebration.

When I catch myself being congruent with my Innate Values, I may say, *I acknowledge myself for living in alignment with my Innate Value of 'Connected.'* Or I might say, *I love the way I honored my Innate Value of 'Free to Express' in the class I just facilitated.*

This Principle affirms that you have consciously noticed that you did in fact live in alignment with one or more of your Innate Values.

Acknowledging and celebrating living in alignment with your Innate Values reinforce your ability to honor who you are meant to be. You have also reinforced that you are capable of creating your own life in a manner that honors your Divine Nature.

Every time you notice and celebrate being your most authentic Self, you are building Self-mastery.

A JOURNEY BACK TO YOUR POSITIVELY BRILLIANT SELF

- Acknowledge yourself for what you did today that was in alignment with your Innate Values.
  - —Be 100% authentic.
  - —*I acknowledge myself for . . .*
- Open up to receive your self-acknowledgment.
  - —Let your self-acknowledgment sink in with a *Thank you.*
  - —When done with humility, this will continue to grow your Self-mastery.
- Repeat this process every time you notice you are living in alignment with one of your Innate Values.

Principle 13: In Her Own Words

✧ You acknowledge and celebrate living in alignment with your Innate Values.

Just How Good Can It Get?

Deb Waterstone

Madison, WI

www.spiritofsuccess.biz

I always wanted my brother to care about me more than he seemed to show. After college, I spent a summer living in his apartment to save money for a backpacking trip. When I left, I said how I appreciated getting closer. He said he didn't feel any closer. Ouch!

Throughout the next 20 years, I went back and forth with my assessment. Just when I felt he truly did care, along would come a major disconnect that reversed my decision. The mixed messages drove me crazy. I felt unloved, and I wasn't sure what I was doing wrong. When I finally asked him about it, I learned that it had more to do with resentments about his upbringing than with me personally, but I still felt the impact of our separation.

A number of years later, I found myself in a workshop on potential and possibilities. At dinner one night, I casually mentioned my relationship with my brother and how I accepted it was as good as it was going to get. Thank goodness they challenged me on this one!

My next step felt bold and scary, but I did it anyway. That very evening, I called my brother and said I wanted a relationship with him that felt connected, real, and honest. I shared what he meant to me, and I emphasized that he didn't need to do one thing differently. I simply wanted to know if he was open to the possibility of having a closer relationship.

This phone call totally transformed our relationship. And it was amazingly simple! Honoring my values helped me reach out, connect from my heart, and open the door to new possibilities for my brother and me.

Today I make a conscious effort to align all aspects of my life with my core values of profound connection, authenticity, fun, freedom, and fluidity.

I've learned that the more aligned I am with these values, the more fulfilled I feel. My deep knowing of these values gives me cause to celebrate every day of my life.

I wonder, just how good can it get?

SECTION IV

Doing Your Innate Life Purpose

When you are inspired by some great purpose,
some extraordinary project, all your thoughts
break their bonds; your mind transcends limitations,
your consciousness expands in every direction,
and you find yourself in a new, great and
wonderful world. Dormant forces, faculties
become alive, and you discover yourself
to be a greater person by far than you
ever dreamed yourself to be.

—Patanjali (c. 1st to 3rd century BC)

In Section IV, Doing Your Innate Life Purpose, you are guided toward knowing, living, and celebrating your Innate Life Purpose.

My Innate Life Purpose is an endowment from my Divine Source. I experience deep inner satisfaction when I consciously remember and live in alignment with my Innate Life Purpose.

What am I doing?

Doing Your Innate Life Purpose is an expression of your Divine Nature through your human nature.

My human nature is curious, industrious, and desirous of connection. My human nature likes 'the act of doing.' But not all doing is as satisfying and fulfilling to my Divine Nature.

Section IV explores the following questions:

1. What is an Innate Life Purpose?
2. Whose purpose are you currently living?
3. Is your doingness rooted in your Divine Nature?
4. Is your doingness rooted in what others have told you is important for you to be doing?

Principle 14

✧ Your Innate Life Purpose is an endowment from your Divine Source.

I know in my heart that man is good, that what is right will always eventually triumph and that there is purpose and worth to each and every life.
—Ronald Reagan

Your Innate Life Purpose is the second endowment from your Divine Source. Your Innate Life Purpose is held as part of your Divine Nature.

Your Innate Life Purpose is the mother lode of foundational Self-discovery. This is the Holy Grail for every human to discover for himself or herself. This single question, "*What is my purpose?*," has weighed heavily on all who seek it.

Think of this as a Divine contract that you are here on Earth to fulfill. In turn, by fulfilling your Innate Life Purpose, you are fulfilled down to the very core of your Positively Brilliant Self.

And, by the way, we all have an Innate Life Purpose. It is also your Divine right to know your own Innate Life Purpose.

I have seen how those I have supported to redis-cover their Innate Life Purpose have taken on new meaning and, in some cases, a new life focus.

Your Divine Nature can only express Itself in this physical world through you as part of your human nature. Your human nature so wants and needs a purpose that without knowing your own Innate Life Purpose your humanness has gravitated to purposes that have been handed to you by others throughout your life. You have been told in varying ways throughout life "*your purpose as a child is to . . .*" or "*your purpose here at work is to . . .*"

While these other purposes have satisfied your ego and have filled your time, they cannot fulfill your Divine Nature's Innate Life Purpose.

A Journey Back to Your Positively Brilliant Self

- What does your inner voice keep calling you to do and contribute?
- What is being revealed?

Principle 14: In His Own Words

✧ Your Innate Life Purpose is an endowment from your Divine Source.

Could It Be Me?

Jeffery G. W. Bow
International Business Coach
Seattle, WA

I thought that being a rebel and looking for causes to channel my anger were in some weird way my quest to help others. This only left me frustrated and unheard.

With no clear direction on what my life purpose was, I thrived on making others happy. I had no time for myself or others close to me and knew this unbalanced life would eventually destroy me.

The foundations that I thought were my supports eventually disappeared, and I was left feeling lost, afraid, and unwanted. However, I ultimately knew inside there was something "more" than my circumstance.

As my life purpose unfolded and I began to under-stand my connection with the Divine, my ability to communicate and connect through the Divine began to flourish.

I started to see the Divine in everyone and everything, and embodied in the concept that we are One.
I realized that, previously, I had created a separation
that was never really there.

My Life Purpose:

**I am here to share with you the gifts that we all
have and to unfold these treasures each and every
day and be in awe of our uniqueness and beauty.
We are inseparable, fluid, and flowing . . . We are
One.**

Now when I begin to feel unbalanced or if I am
looking at a new project, I reflect back to my life purpose
and use that as my guide and reminder. I now make a
decision based on how it serves my life purpose and life's
work using me as a conduit to the Divine.

My life's work allows me to make a positive impact
on someone's life every day. Now when I work through
my life purpose, I am happy and satisfied, and at peace.

Principle 15

✧ You know your Innate Life Purpose.

> *The purpose of life*
> *is a life of purpose.*
> —Robert Byrne

What a brilliant statement to be able to make: "I know my Innate Life Purpose." To say this is breathtaking. This means you have cut through what others have told you about your purpose in life. You have gone back to reconnect with your Divine Nature, to your infinite resourcefulness to gain an understanding of what your unique purpose is.

Discovering one's real Life Purpose is sometimes held, even by the most conscious and personally responsible people I have known, to be a daunting and serious matter.

I invite you to take a relaxing deep breath; finding your own Innate Life Purpose does not have to be a scary or even a challenging Self-discovery journey.

How do you know what you are receiving is from your Divine Nature and that it is your Innate Life Purpose? Here are some of the criteria I used for myself and for many I have supported to access and articulate their Innate Life Purpose.

- Was its origin from deep inside me, from my Divine Nature?
- Is it life-affirming?
- Is it deeply and personally compelling?

My Innate Life Purpose statement:

I am the exquisite and playful orchestration of my unique human expression and my oneness with Spirit that come together to create a bodacious flourishing of life!

Other sample Innate Life Purpose statements:

I am the safe harbor that invites all seekers of peace to reflect, rest, and replenish!

I am the sage who sees and celebrates your wisdom!

A JOURNEY BACK TO YOUR POSITIVELY BRILLIANT SELF

- What is your Innate Life Purpose?
- What are you here to do, and contribute?
- What are you naturally passionate about?
- What are you doing when you notice your heart and soul singing for joy?
- Who are you here to serve?

Principle 15: In His Own Words

✧ You know your Innate Life Purpose.

Aligning with Your Heart

Robert Stack, MCLC, APR, Fellow PRSA

FAME COACH®

Palm Beach Gardens, FL

www.famecoach.com

It was not until I suffered a myocardial infarction and underwent emergency cardiac bypass surgery in April 1995 at the age of 38 that I began to ponder the powerful inquiry, "Is there a larger purpose for living?" After coming so close to my death and miraculously surviving, I struggled with mortality issues and a life that had been turned upside down.

Until my heart attack, I was a respected industry leader in the entertainment field, who represented prominent CEOs, sports celebrities, and Hollywood superstars. After my open-heart surgery, I lost total confidence in myself. Furthermore, I began to question my career path and struggled to save my relationship with my girlfriend, who was enduring a messy divorce.

Paraphrasing comments by Dan Millman in his book Living on Purpose, *I was living my life by accident, stumbling into relationships, wandering into careers, searching for deeper meaning, hoping and praying that I'd get lucky in love, find my fortune, and avoid another heart attack. I now realize that I lived the first four decades of my life at random, not on purpose.*

My decision to become a professional life coach started me down a transformational path of Self-mastery that deepened my understanding of how to live on purpose. During my coach training several years ago, I birthed a life purpose statement that continues to serve me: **I am giving unconditionally with my heart and in awe of the wondrous process of Self-mastery as I learn to harness my spirituality and unique gift of guiding others on the path of life by being a stellar role model**.

As a direct result of knowing my life purpose, I am proud to say I am a leader and trendsetter in both the coaching and speaking professions. Overcoming seemingly impossible odds and a mountain of adversity, I am living life according to my innate life purpose by aligning what I do with my heart.

I owe my personal comeback, in part, to my steadfast determination to discover my life purpose and the realization that the answers I am seeking are within me. I just needed to open myself up to what's inside and authentically live it.

No one should have to suffer a heart attack to learn a lesson, but I did. I learned to honor my heart, because my heart knows the way.

Principle 16

✧ You live in alignment with your Innate Life Purpose.

*I am here for a purpose
and that purpose is to grow into a mountain,
not to shrink to a grain of sand.
Henceforth will I apply all my efforts
to become the highest mountain of all and
I will strain my potential until it cries for mercy.*
—Og Mandino

Now that you know your Innate Life Purpose, what are you going to do with this knowledge? As a human being, you have a choice. Just because you know something doesn't mean that you are ready, willing, or able to act upon or integrate what you know into your personal or professional life. Here is another opportunity to give yourself the permission to just be with your newly acquired insight. It is a good thing to take time to reflect.

When you are ready, you will know it is time to align your daily life with what has been revealed to you by your Divine Nature in the form of your Innate Life Purpose.

Innate Life Purpose - the 'mother lode of insights'

I refer to this as the 'mother lode of insights' because your Innate Life Purpose answers or directly informs all of these related questions:

- *Why am I alive?*
- *What is my purpose for living my life now?*
- *What is my life all about?*
- *Who am I here to serve?*
- *How am I to make a difference?*
- *What is my life's work?*
- *What vision am I to bring to my world?*

The answer to this single question, "What is my Innate Life Purpose?" guides you to answer all of these questions.

When you are fulfilling your Innate Life Purpose, you experience:

- Being passionate about your work
- Time standing still and flying by unnoticed at the same time
- Insights into your work that you cannot know from previous experiences or study
- Profound humility by your capacity to do what you are doing
- Serving or contributing to a higher quality of peace, life, love, acceptance, or unity for someone other than yourself

Can you imagine living in alignment with your Innate Life Purpose? I'll have more of this!

The alignment process is quite simple.

View each issue, project, decision, or opportunity through the lens of your Innate Life Purpose. With a little practice, it becomes very clear: this choice is or is not aligned with my Innate Life Purpose.

My experience with this simple yet significant process is an unimaginable freedom to know when it is right for me to say yes or no to everything that comes to me. Remember, my history was one where I was a people-pleaser. Before really knowing my own Innate Life Purpose, I felt compelled to say *yes* to what people wanted from me to help them with their purpose.

By knowing and aligning with my own Innate Life Purpose, I can easily say *no* to 'bright ideas' my ego comes up with. I can reflect through my Innate Life Purpose to determine, "*Is this aligned with my Innate Life Purpose?*"

My Innate Life Purpose is: *I am the exquisite and playful orchestration of my unique human expression and my oneness with Spirit that come together to create a bodacious flourishing of life.*

My ego's purpose has been: *I am the supporter for anyone at work who asks me to do something that will further my employer's purposes.* I have found that my ego's purpose or 'bright ideas' are distractions.

Other questions I use to align my life with my Innate Life Purpose:

- *Is this my work to do?*
- *Am I really passionate about this opportunity?*
- *Which action or decision honors my Innate Life Purpose?*
- *Am I being the best steward of my Innate Life Purpose by being part of this project?*

A JOURNEY BACK TO YOUR POSITIVELY BRILLIANT SELF

- What issue or opportunity do you have today?
- Based on your knowledge of what your Innate Life Purpose is, what would serve you and your Innate Life Purpose in this matter?
- Is this your work to do? [Note: The question here is not "Is this worthwhile work?"]
- Are you passionate about this?

Principle 16: In Her Own Words

✧ You live in alignment with your Innate Life Purpose.

Creativity in Action

    Kay Richardson, MFT, CLC

    San Diego, CA

    www.kayrichardson.com

"To whom much is given, much is required." For me, Jesus' words were serious fuel for the growing internal pressure I'd created by the time I was 13. I felt I had to do something big and meaningful in the world . . . preferably yesterday.

I pursued the healing and performing arts, and my creative passions grew exponentially: therapy, facilitating, singing, acting, dance, coaching, writing. . . . So add overwhelmed to the internal pressure, and by midlife, I was ready to explode. Which was my highest path?

Fortunately, divine guidance came in several ways. First, my grandmother offered compassionate advice: "Take the pressure off!" When I allowed myself some breathing room, a new view began to emerge. During a Narrative Therapy conference, I was struck by the question, "Are you living out of your preferred identity?" I knew immediately the identity I love most: artist (of many forms).

As I explored this integrated sense of identity as artist, another flash of insight came: "creativity in action." This captures who I am and all I've done, and when I include the meaningful connections I make as I express from my heart, my Innate Life Purpose is clear—**I am creativity in action, inspiring transcendent exchange through heartfelt expression.**

I felt tremendous relief in committing to my chosen purpose. I realized all I create adds up to be my meaningful contribution to the world within this clarifying framework. I've lived in alignment with my Innate Life Purpose all along!

When I sing from my heart, I experience that higher-level connection with the audience, a transcendent exchange. This is the essence I also love in coaching, writing, or any form my creativity may take. I now enjoy a daily practice of noticing all the ways I'm being "creativity in action." And this week I received a Maya Angelou quote as confirmation: "I believe in living a poetic life, an art full life. Everything we do is part of a large canvas upon which we are creating our own art."

Principle 17

✧ You acknowledge and celebrate living in alignment with your Innate Life Purpose.

The more you praise and celebrate your life,
the more there is in life to celebrate.
—Oprah Winfrey

Knowing your Innate Life Purpose is the "mother lode of insights" for anyone seeking Self-mastery.

Acknowledging yourself for living your Innate Life Purpose is to "live heaven on earth." Can you imagine your life being lived on purpose, and not just any purpose but your Innate Life Purpose? Can you feel yourself become more empowered in this moment as you dare to imagine such a life?

First, you realize that you have chosen to know your own Innate Life Purpose. Second, you live in alignment with your Innate Life Purpose. There are surges of energy inherent in living in congruence with your most masterful Self. Now, it is time to celebrate. By acknowledging and celebrating living in alignment with your Innate Life Purpose you expand your capacity to be and do even more of your authentic Self.

Acknowledgment and celebration are essential parts of Self-mastery because they strengthen your human nature's need for knowing that you are on track and you are capable of creating your life to be on purpose.

Continuing acknowledgment and celebration based on real, observable evidence of Self-mastery also keep the doubts and limiting beliefs from creeping back into our human nature's ego mind. Acknowledgment is the antidote to mass consciousness's barrage and your own limiting self-talk of, "*Who do you think you are?*" and "*You can't change the world.*"

I bring a celebration of gratitude and humility when I realize that I am living in alignment with my Innate Life Purpose. Thank you, Divine Source.

A JOURNEY BACK TO YOUR POSITIVELY BRILLIANT SELF

- Begin to look for where and when you are already living in alignment with your Innate Life Purpose.
- Acknowledge your Self. "*I acknowledge myself for…*"
- Receive your self-acknowledgement with a simple and grateful "*Thank you.*"

Principle 17: In Her Own Words

✧ You acknowledge and celebrate living in alignment with your Innate Life Purpose.

Loving Myself First . . . What a Concept!

Jodi Anthony, CLC, Certified Life Coach

Ventura, CA

www.LifeCoachingWithJodi.com

Four years ago, if someone had told me that to truly love others, I would have to start by loving myself first, I would have looked at that person like he was crazy… how do I do that?

Until recently, I always lived my life helping others before I helped myself. It always felt better to focus on other people first. If they were happy, then I was happy.

Four years ago, my marriage fell apart, and I was devastated. I had two young children, and I was overwhelmed. I wasn't sure where to begin, but I knew that I had to do something radically different.

What I didn't know during this dark time was that the most amazing journey was about to unfold. After signing up for various workshops, I got to see through other people's eyes that I was a pretty amazing person. There was nothing that I had to fix, and there was nothing broken. What I began to do was to love myself unconditionally. For the first time in my life, I could see that I don't need to do or be anything else… I am enough.

Through this experience, I discovered that my life purpose is to love myself unconditionally and claim God's perfection in me and to help others see their own magnificence and claim it for themselves.

Now I get to coach others and reflect back their magnificence wherever I see it and then sit back and witness the miracle of them loving themselves unconditionally.

I am so passionate about helping others claim their magnificence. What I realize now is that I couldn't have gotten here without claiming it for myself first.

Section V

Using Your Innate Gifts

Our talents are the gift that God gives to us…What we make of our talents is our gift back to God.
—Leo Buscaglia

In Section V, Using Your Innate Gifts, you are guided toward knowing, living, and celebrating your Innate Gifts.

We use, grow, strengthen, and, in some cases, master some skills and talents. But are these skills and talents that we have worked so hard at our Innate Gifts?

In many cases, I find that my clients and students know one or two of their Innate Gifts, and have employed these gifts in their lives. But even these are not fully employed or integrated into their lives. Sadly, I have not met anyone who fully knows, appreciates, and is using the full power of his or her Divinely endowed Innate Gifts before a personal and conscious journey into himself or herself.

During my lifetime, there has been a higher level of public awareness of not wasting our Earth's natural resources than there has been of not squandering our own Divinely endowed resources in the form of our Innate Gifts.

Where is the world's outrage about each of us squandering our Innate Gifts by not fully knowing, developing, using, and celebrating them?

There are full-fledged public campaigns to understand the impact of how we use (and abuse) our natural worldly resources. I have personally benefited from these public campaigns.

I would also applaud and welcome a similar or even bigger campaign to raise the level of awareness of the vast and mostly untapped natural resources that lies within each of us.

What do you know about your own personal resources in the form of your Innate Gifts?

The cumulative effect of not using our Innate Gifts is a world filled with frustration rather than fulfillment and a world filled with broken hearts rather than joyous hearts. This spills into every family unit, community, and organization.

By each of us not knowing and living our Positively Brilliant Selves, we have collectively created world-wide epidemics of shortage, lack, and waste. The great news is, since we each had a hand in creating these epidemics, we can each choose to do something about them. I will go one step further. Each of us is the only one who can do this work for our Selves, and by transforming our Selves, we transform the world.

We become happier and more productive by living our own lives and using our own Innate Gifts. Simultaneously, by using our own Innate Gifts, we contribute our best and brightest to our part of the world. Our part of the world literally becomes a better place to live, for us as well as for those we are here to serve.

For the past 15 years, I have been consciously employing my Innate Gifts of *Creating safe space, Listening with honor, Championing, Facilitating magnificence, Loving, Seeing the best in everyone, Seeing conceptually, and Communicating complex concepts so others can understand.*

As a direct result, I have touched thousands with the Principles contained in this book. I know I have made a significant and positive contribution to those I am here to serve. By using my Innate Gifts in service of my Innate Life Purpose while honoring my Innate Values, I am contributing my very best to my part of the world.

SECTION V EXPLORES THE FOLLOWING QUESTIONS:

1. Do you really know, live, and celebrate your own Innate Gifts?
2. What Innate Gifts are you ready to use more frequently?
3. What Innate Gifts are you ready to further develop?

Principle 18

✦ Your Innate Gifts are an endowment from your Divine Source.

Help me to master my skills so that I may place them in your service so that I may fulfill my purpose here. Allow me to complete my work on earth with care and humility and return to you when my work here is done. May all veils and barriers that separate us dissolve so that I may dwell fully and completely in your love...Amen!
—Paul Ferinni

Innate Gifts are the third endowment from your Divine Source. Your Innate Gifts are part of your Divine Nature. My human nature has access to and is the steward of my Innate Gifts.

Innate Gifts are given as a life-long endowment. They are not earned or awarded for any particular behavior. Innate Gifts can never be taken away. They can, however, collect dust, be put on a shelf, and perhaps even be forgotten about by the person endowed.

Your Innate Gifts will forever remain available to you to be remembered, developed, and used to help fulfill your Innate Life Purpose.

For a good part of my life, I was told what I had to learn and what skills were mandatory to be successful. I spent many decades of hard work developing skills and knowledge in areas of business management, finance, and systems infrastructure. Before moving to Tokyo, Japan, I took intensive Japanese language training one-on-one with a Japanese tutor.

I gained a learned-mastery in each of these skill areas, and they served me in the corporate world. But as I reflect on the massive time and energy I invested in mastering these skills, I realize I never got to a level of natural mastery, and I did not feel deeply fulfilled.

On the other hand, developing my Innate Gifts has been satisfying and joyful. Mastery has come easily, and employing my Innate Gifts is as natural as breathing.

A Journey Back to Your Positively Brilliant Self

- What are your Innate Gifts?
- What natural talents seem like second nature?
- Which Innate Gift needs more nurturing, now?

Principle 18: In His Own Words

✦ Your Innate Gifts are an endowment from your Divine Source.

A Lifelong Burden Turns Out to be a God-given Gift
Peter J. Reding, Master Certified Coach
San Diego, CA
www.coachforlife.com

As a child, I was the primary listener for my mother. In my teens and 20s, I listened to my peers more than I spoke. Into my 30s and 40s, I was amazed at how insensitive many people were when they shared their opinion or judgment that slammed one or more of the people in the group. And the person sharing didn't seem to even notice the impact on those he verbally put down.

In my late 30s and early 40s, I began to feel burdened by listening so deeply. Why do I hear things that others do not? Am I to point out to all the insensitive individuals to be more thoughtful in their sharing?

I couldn't stop myself listening at a deep, intuitive, honoring and compassionate level.

I had always been a good mediator because my keen listening skills allowed me to really hear what was important to each person. I could also hear the underlying nuances, motivations, and aspirations that were tied to each person's position or belief.

Even though I was (and still am) great at mediation, I did not enjoy being in the constant environment of conflict and argument. In this environment, listening still felt like a burden.

In my late 40s, I was introduced to the newly forming profession of personal life coaching. **My gift of deep, compassionate, and intuitive listening with honor** turns out to be the premier competency to be a masterful life coach!

I looked back over my life to realize I had been a gifted listener my whole life. I have been developing my natural gift of listening since birth.

My natural and powerful gift of listening is no longer a burden as a coach. Rather than being in an environment of conflict, I am now listening for what my clients want to create. I can hear my clients' vision, passions, aspirations, strengths, values, purpose, and yes, their own unique, God-given gifts.

Principle 19

✧ You know your Innate Gifts.

As simple as it sounds,
we all must try to be the best person we can:
by making the best choices,
by making the most of the talents we've been given.
—Mary Lou Retton

Do you know what your Innate Gifts are? You initially received Innate Gifts at birth, maybe even at your conception. They may or may not be developed; that part is up to your human nature's free will.

The identification and development of gifts other than our Innate Gifts is often dictated by the culture in which we grow up. Our parents' beliefs about who they want us to be influence and guide what skills and talents we should pursue to be successful or happy.

Developing other gifts, skills or talents do not come as naturally or easily as the development of our own Innate Gifts. It takes concerted effort to improve other skills, and using these talents do not provide an inner satisfaction or sense of fulfillment. I call these "learned talents."

Examples of my learned talents

Business, Negotiating, Writing contracts, Systems-infra-structure, Learning foreign languages, and Networking

Knowing your Innate Gifts supports you to fully develop them. You have to develop them in order to grow your full personal capacity and most valuable resources to fulfill your Innate Life Purpose.

When you develop learned talents, you are restricting yourself. Think of your Innate Gifts as the power tools you have been provided to do your unique work or make your unique contribution to your world. Think of your learned talents as the arduous hand tools that continue to give you blisters.

You may be thinking, *"I have developed several skills, to become very successful at what I do."* I, too, earlier in my life developed many learned talents to the point of working competency and some to a level of high proficiency. Those learned talents provided me a lot of material success. And the price I paid for developing these learned talents was an investment of extraordinary effort, time, and energy.

Was all this time spent developing my learned talents wasted? No, not completely. All of my experiences and learning got me to where I am today. Would knowing my Innate Gifts earlier in life have served me better? The answer to this question will never be known. For me, when I was ready to know, I knew.

At this point in your life, the question becomes, *"What Innate Gifts are within you that you have been ignoring in favor of developing what the outside world has told you to develop?"* By choosing to really know and develop your Innate Gifts, you can begin to fully use your Innate Gifts to make the greatest contribution you can during the rest of your life. This conscious choice to know and develop your Innate Gifts also brings a deep and enduring fulfillment. The road to Self-mastery must travel through the land of knowing your own Innate Gifts.

The alternative is to stick to previously learned talents that, at the very best, will provide physical comforts. However, a natural and easy Self-mastery can never be obtained.

My Innate Gifts:

Creating safe space, Listening with honor, Championing, Facilitating magnificence, Loving, Seeing the best in everyone, Seeing conceptually, and Communicating complex concepts so others can understand

Knowing my Innate Gifts was my first step in the Self-mastery cycle of knowing, living, and celebrating my own Innate Gifts. I now have the clarity to employ more of my Innate Gifts in my daily work and certainly in my life's work. Life has become easier.

Learning and further developing my Innate Gifts feel more natural. My curiosities run parallel with my Innate Gifts. I also find that I learn and master competencies that are congruent with my Innate Gifts more quickly.

A JOURNEY BACK TO YOUR POSITIVELY BRILLIANT SELF

- What have you always loved to do?
- What has always come easily, naturally?
- What can you spend hours on without knowing the time?
- What gifts or talents do you most admire in your heroes, fictional or real?
- What can you do really well that you have never been taught to do?

Principle 19: In Her Own Words

✦ You know your Innate Gifts.

A Little Detective Work

Bonnie Leonard, EdD, CLC

Midlife Coach for Women

North Kingstown, RI

www.bonnieleonard.com

Not so fast here! There are some real challenges in discerning our innate gifts. They come so automatically for us that it's usually difficult to see them.

As a child, I was aware of those talents that won approval from my parents and teachers. I observed my father's and grandmother's pleasure at school achievement, so I became one of those top-of-the-class kids. Since all my relatives remarked on what a "good little mother" I was, I also took this talent to heart.

But once I completed my coach-training courses, I realized the importance of determining my natural gifts on a more conscious level, so I did some detective work on my own behalf. First, I took the StrengthsFinder® Profile in Now, Discover Your Strengths *by Buckingham and Clifton. I selected three of the top strengths revealed there:* **Connectedness, Empathy, and Learner***. These felt immediately right* to me - especially **Connectedness**, which is the ability to see that all things are connected. I also couldn't help but notice that sensing the emotions around you (**Empathy**) is a skill involved in mothering and that a love of learning (**Learner**) probably provided a great basis for school achievement.

Then I honed in on those faculties I employ instinctively and added **Organization** to my list. (If I enter a situation that feels "off," I cannot help but do a quick read and make mental changes that will allow things to flow more smoothly.) **Creating** also made the list, because if I'm inspired, I'll start a creative project on the spot—I mean, right then!

The next step in my sleuthing adventure was to note commentary from family and friends about possible talents. Over the years, so many people have told me how much they love my laugh that I had to annex **Laughter**.

So, with a little bit of investigative work, I determined that my gifts are **Connectedness, Empathy, Learner, Organization, Creating and Laughter**. The happy outcome is that when I engage these innate talents, I enter a state of flow where time has no place and delight abounds. And who doesn't want some of that?

Principle 20

✧ You live in alignment with your Innate Gifts.

The person born with a talent they are meant to use will find their greatest happiness in using it.
—Johann Wolfgang von Goethe

Now that you know your Innate Gifts, you have a choice as to how, when, and where you will develop and use these Gifts. Your Innate Gifts can now be employed to fulfill your Innate Life Purpose, which, in turn, contributes to serving your world.

When I focused on developing other skills that were not rooted in my Innate Gifts I wasted energy, was mostly frustrated, and ultimately unfulfilled. When I began to develop and use my Innate Gifts, many that had been dormant, my 'work' shifted to contribution and my busy-ness shifted to fulfillment.

Aligning your life choices and actions with your Innate Gifts is very simple. With practice, it can even be easy. Do not get discouraged initially if the aligning process seems uncomfortable or unsupported by others who are vested in you to remain as you have been. There may be those who want you to continue to use your learned talents for their own acquired taste of what your learned talents have produced and continue to produce.

Aligning my life and life's work with my Innate Gifts has been an easy and gradual process. As I continue to open to Divine Nature's guidance on what projects align with my Innate Life Purpose, my Innate Gifts have surfaced organically. The skills that I have needed to accomplish the projects that make up my Innate Life Purpose have all been contained in my Innate Gifts.

A Journey Back to Your Positively Brilliant Self

The alignment process

- Note the largest blocks of activity where you spend your time at work and at home.
  - —What learned talents are you using to accomplish these activities?
  - —What Innate Gifts are you using to accomplish these activities?
- How much of your Innate Gifts are being used?
- How can you incorporate more of your Innate Gifts into your current life?

Principle 20: In Her Own Words

✧ You live in alignment with your Innate Gifts.

I Can Get Paid to Do This?

Karen Dimmick, Speaker, Mentor, Trainer

Fort Collins, CO

Taking Entrepreneurs from Passions to Profit

www.AwakeningInsight.com

"Wow, thanks, I never thought of it that way!" was the one thing I heard the most from friends at high school, college, and then work. I seemed to have a knack for explaining things easily and inspiring people to go for what they wanted.

The trouble was, I didn't know what I wanted to do, because I really wasn't inspired by the things I was "good at" at school.

I went straight into a very prestigious job from college, and within a couple of months, I realized it wasn't for me. Pretty soon, I started my own business and consulted for some of the top 100 companies in the world. However, nothing seemed to fulfill me, so I kept moving on.

In my spare time, I was the person everyone came to for personal help and advice. All of them seemed to go away energized, having found the answers they needed. I, on the other hand, seemed to be getting further and further away from being fulfilled.

After several huge life changes, **I discovered my gifts: an intuitive passion for business and the ability to inspire and empower entrepreneurs to achieve their dreams.** I found that the insights I gave could literally turn people's businesses around, which in turn is allowing them to change the world!

Finally I was feeling fulfilled because I knew my gifts and I was using my gifts as they were meant to be used. I am on the way to my dream of a world of passionate entrepreneurs.

I now employ my gift of **empowering** by training service-based entrepreneurs to go from passions to profit and my gift of **inspiring** to help them achieve their life purposes.

As I speak and train, I feel so full of life. I am literally walking on air, and my excitement bubbles over into everyone around me.

Principle 21

✧ You acknowledge and celebrate living in alignment with your Innate Gifts.

> *When you use*
> *one or more of your Innate Gifts*
> *you feel a deep exhilaration and,*
> *at the very same moment,*
> *profound humility.*
> —Peter J. Reding

Celebration is having a good time. Celebrating your most essential Self-mastery by fully living in alignment with your Innate Gifts is awe-inspiring. It may be more accurate to define this Principle as the authentic celebration of your Divine Nature being lived through your human nature. How glorious is this?

The acknowledging and celebrating contained in this Principle are not the *'look at me, I am so great and doing better than you'* variety.

The acknowledging and celebrating contained in this Principle are the *'I am so blessed, so grateful, and so humbled to be in a place where I know my Innate Gifts, and I am bringing my Innate Gifts to my Innate Life Purpose'* variety.

Can you imagine being and doing exactly what you are here to do at this time, in this place and with these people? This honors your Divine Nature's expression. This is the deepest and most satisfying fulfillment you can experience. You are experiencing Self-mastery.

The act of acknowledging and celebrating the fact that you are living in alignment with your Innate Gifts provides a surge to know your Self even better, to live your Self more fully, and to celebrate your Self more.

There are small and large ways I celebrate living my own life. I celebrate living in alignment with my Innate Gifts of *'creating safe space, seeing the best in everyone, communicating complex concepts so others can understand, and championing'* by authoring and publishing the *Positively Brilliant Self-mastery Series*.

A JOURNEY BACK TO YOUR POSITIVELY BRILLIANT SELF

- What Innate Gift did you use today?
- What did you contribute to your world today that used one of your Innate Gifts?
- Celebrate and acknowledge yourself for living in alignment with your Innate Gifts.

Principle 21: In His Own Words

✦ You acknowledge and celebrate living in alignment with your Innate Gifts.

More Than a Positive Approach
Larry Williamson, MCC, MCLC
Rocky Mount, NC
Anchored Values Coaching and Consulting®
www.anchoredvalues.com

I have always approached life with a joyful and positive attitude. This was important to me. It was, and is, real. I liked the way it helped me bounce back from challenges, and I enjoyed watching the impact my positive attitude had on others. I worked hard to focus on and was committed to developing this trait. Why was I working so hard on something that seemed so natural?

I charged forward, first in one direction, and then in another, always applying my positive approach and attitude. I successfully took on challenges and worked hard on the many requests "presented by others." Trying to live my life in accordance with the expectations of others, my successes were short lived and brought about much struggle. I remained unsatisfied. I knew there must be something more.

I was presented many opportunities to attend development seminars and programs, was introduced to many wonderful books on personal growth, and was honored to work closely with many wise teachers. I learned to look inward, to self-examine, and to be honest with myself.

I began to realize I was never more content than when I used my gift of **connecting with and supporting others on a personal level.** I also discovered my gift of **being able to sit comfortably with others and through our conversation watch as they began to see clearly through and beyond the challenges they faced**.

As a life coach, I delight in watching the people I support gain clarity and insight into their current situation, determine their true desires, create their visions, and then celebrate their successes with them.

My focus is now aligned with my gifts and talents of **holding a positive approach and supporting others on a personal level**. As a direct result, I have never been more content and more energized by what I do. And when I am living in alignment with my gifts I no longer have to "work" on my positive attitude!

And There's More

This is the foundational book for the *Positively Brilliant Self-mastery Series™*. I have described a simple yet profound foundation to guide you back to your most authentic Self. While this book is simple and easy to understand, rereading this book will surely bring even more insights and greater Self-mastery.

This book sets the foundational stage for you to engage in deeper and more personal work to explore your own inner world. You have been endowed by your Divine Source with a Divine Nature that holds the treasures of Innate Values, an Innate Life Purpose, and Innate Gifts. The balance of the *Positively Brilliant Self-mastery Series* is your key to help you unlock the life that only you can live.

Each of the soon to be released *Positively Brilliant Self-mastery – Workshop in a Box™* offerings will consist of:

- A detailed step-by-step workbook
- Audio tracks to support self-exploration
- Audio tracks to support integration
- A Positively Brilliant Self-mastery Assessment™
- Positively Brilliant Group Guidelines™
- A Positively Brilliant Mastery Journal™

Each *Positively Brilliant Self-mastery - Workshop in a Box* supports your discovery, integration, tracking, and celebration of your Positively Brilliant Self.

Positively Brilliant Self-mastery Workshop in a Box #1

A Guided Journey Back to Your Life-affirming Divine Nature

Positively Brilliant Self-mastery Workshop in a Box #2

A Guided Journey Back to Your Life-affirming Human Nature

Positively Brilliant Self-mastery Workshop in a Box #3

A Guided Journey Back to Your Innate Values

Positively Brilliant Self-mastery Workshop in a Box #4

A Guided Journey Back to Your Innate Life Purpose

Positively Brilliant Self-mastery Workshop in a Box #5

A Guided Journey Back to Your Innate Gifts

www.positivelybrilliant.com

Section I – Your Infinite Divine Nature

Principle 1: *"I Heard Myself Say . . ."*
Ann Ranson
Dallas, TX
Inspired Business Models
www.annranson.com

Principle 2: *Problems or Gifts?*
Scott Bogart, Author and Life Coach
Ventura, CA

Principle 3: *I Choose Now...and Now...and Now...*
LeAnn Riley, Realtor and Master Coach
Minneapolis, MN
www.affluentchoice.com

Section II – Your Creative Human Nature

Principle 4: *Becoming Spaciousness*
Jennifer Sellers, CEO, Coach
Inspired Mastery
Tucson, AZ
www.inspiredmastery.com

Principle 5: *Can I Be Myself Already?*
Phyliss Francis, PCC, Professional Certified Coach,
Speaker
Honolulu, HI
www.awakeninglives.com

Principle 6: *How My Fallback Plan Sabotaged My Authenticity*
Steve Dimmick, Mentor to Passionate Entrepreneurs
Fort Collins, CO
www.AwakeningInsight.com

Principle 7: *Am I Too Different to Be Loved?*
Marc A. Carignan, President & CEO
Life Success Strategies, Inc.
San Diego, CA
www.lifesuccessstrategies.com

Principle 8: *It All Comes Down to ME!*
Sheri Boone, MCC, CLC, Inspired Mastery
Portland, OR
www.inspiredmastery.com
www.mccmentorcoach.com

Principle 9: *My Kids Are Smarter Than I Thought*
Allen R. Valencour, Professional Certified Coach
CEO, Off Field Coaching, Inc.®
Prescott Valley, AZ
al@offfieldcoaching.com

Section III – Being Your Innate Values

Principle 10: *My Values Influence My Thoughts, Behaviors, and Actions*
Marcy Johnsrude, Inspired Coach, Consultant, Trainer, Author, and Writer
Nanaimo, British Columbia

Principle 11: *Memory's First Love*
Bonnie Leonard, EdD, CLC
Bonnie is a Midlife Coach for women in transition. As a former Dean of Continuing Education at Wellesley College and certified Life Coach, she has helped hundreds of women find that "more inside" and reinvent their lives. All Bonnie's clients begin their coaching work with the Compasswise™ Program, where she guides them through a self-discovery adventure to find their true Gifts, Passions, Values and Purpose. You can learn more by visiting www.bonnieleonard.com.

Principle 12: *My Life as an Old Typewriter*
Caryn McCurry, Inspirer of Choice
New York, NY
www.singularitynyc.com

Principle 13: *Just How Good Can It Get?*
Deb Waterstone
Madison, WI
www.spiritofsuccess.biz

Section IV – Doing Your Innate Life Purpose

Principle 14: *Could It Be Me?*
Jeffery G. W. Bow, International Business Coach
Seattle, WA

Principle 15: *Aligning with Your Heart*
Robert Stack, MCLC, APR, Fellow PRSA,
FAME COACH®
Palm Beach Gardens, FL
www.famecoach.com

Principle 16: *Creativity in Action*
Kay Richardson, MFT, CLC
San Diego, CA
www.kayrichardson.com

Principle 17: *Loving Myself First…What a Concept!*
Jodi Anthony, CLC, Certified Life Coach
Ventura, CA
www.LifeCoachingWithJodi.com

Section V – Using Your Innate Gifts

Principle 18: *A Lifelong Burden Turns Out to be a God-given Gift*
Peter J. Reding, Master Certified Coach
San Diego, CA
www.coachforlife.com

Principle 19: *A Little Detective Work*
Bonnie Leonard, EdD, CLC
Bonnie is a Midlife Coach for women in transition. As a former Dean of Continuing Education at Wellesley College and certified Life Coach, she has helped hundreds of women find that "more inside" and reinvent their lives. All Bonnie's clients begin their coaching work with the Compasswise™ Program, where she guides them through a self-discovery adventure to find their true Gifts, Passions, Values and Purpose. You can learn more by visiting www.bonnieleonard.com.

Principle 20: *I Can Get Paid to Do This?*
Karen Dimmick, Speaker, Mentor, Trainer
Fort Collins, CO
www.AwakeningInsight.com

Principle 21: *More Than a Positive Approach*
Larry Williamson, MCC, MCLC
Rocky Mount, NC
www.anchoredvalues.com

Positively Brilliant Books and Self-study Programs

For future Positively Brilliant books, audio books, visualization CDs, and journals, please visit:
www.positivelybrilliant.com

Positively Brilliant Series products are designed as guided, self-discovery journeys using multi-sensory, step-by-step, interactive, and self-paced tools. These products are for every person who wants to know:

- Do I have a Divine Source? And how do I connect with It?
- What are life-affirming beliefs and attitudes?
- What do I stand for? What are my values?
- Why am I here? What is my purpose?
- What God-given gifts have I been endowed with?

And . . .

- How do I find these deep answers within me?
- How can I practically integrate all of this in my daily life?

POSITIVELY BRILLIANT SERVICES

Positively Brilliant Series services are offered to support, inspire, and reinforce your Positively Brilliant Self.

Begin or Join a Positively Brilliant Group
- Positively Brilliant Study Group™
    - —Free Positively Brilliant Study Group Guidelines™
    - —Creating a positive learning environment for your study group
    - —**www.positivelybrilliant.com**
- Positively Brilliant Master Mind Group™
    - —Free Positively Brilliant Master Mind Group Guidelines™
    - —Creating a positive and supportive environment for your Master Mind
    - —**www.positivelybrilliant.com**

Track your Positively Brilliant Mastery
- Free Positively Brilliant Self-Assessments™
- **www.positivelybrilliant.com**

Contribute a Positively Brilliant Story
- Free Positively Brilliant Story Template™
- **www.positivelybrilliant.com**

Accredited Life Coach Training and Certification

Coach For Life – www.coachforlife.com

Peter J. Reding co-founded Coach For Life in 1996. Coach For Life offers two International Coach Federation (ICF) Accredited Coach Training Programs (ACTP).

The Spiritually-based principles in this book were developed at Coach For Life and are taught as part of the *Fulfillment Coaching Model*™. The coaches we have taught and certified since 1996 are among the most holistic and Spiritual coaches in the coaching profession today.

Facilitator Training and Certification

The Foundation for Inspired Learning
www.inspiredlearning.org

Peter J. Reding founded the Foundation for Inspired Learning in 2003 as a 501(c)3 nonprofit.

The Foundation for Inspired Learning offers a powerful, acknowledgment-based learning philosophy that is articulated in secular terms so any school, business, or organization can implement it. Certification is offered in the *Inspired Learning Model*™.

Peter J. Reding's Positively Brilliant Self

My Divine Nature:
- *I am one with my Divine Nature.*
- *I have direct access to my Divine Source.*

My human nature:
- *I consciously choose life-affirming beliefs.*
- *I consciously choose life-affirming attitudes.*

My Innate Values:
Creative, Connected, Thriving, Retreat, and Free to Express.

My Innate Life Purpose:
I am the exquisite and playful orchestration of my unique human expression and my oneness with Spirit that come together to create a bodacious flourishing of life.

My Innate Gifts:
Creating safe space, Listening with honor, Championing, Facilitating magnificence, Loving, Seeing the best in everyone, Seeing conceptually, and Communicating complex concepts so others can understand.

Peter J. Reding - Traditional Education:
- BS – Marquette University
- MBA – Pepperdine University
- MCC – Master Certified Coach, International Coach Federation **www.coachfederation.org**

Peter J. Reding - Organizations Founded

Coach For Life, Co-founder
- **http://www.coachforlife.com**
- Spiritually-based, Accredited Coach Training

Foundation for Inspired Learning, Founder
- **http://www.inspiredlearning.org**
- 501(c)3, teaching and certifying facilitators of learning in the *Inspired Learning Model*™
- The co-originator and author of the *Inspired Learning Model*™ *Handbook*

Positively Brilliant, LLC, Founder
- **http://www.positivelybrilliant.com**
- The *Positively Brilliant Series*™

Positively Brilliant Productions, Founder
- **www.positivelybrilliantproductions.com**
- Publisher of the *Positively Brilliant Series*™
- Producer of *Positively Brilliant Events*™